CW01334424

A HISTORY OF HAMPSTHWAITE

BOOK 1:

VILLAGERS' REMINISCENCES

Edited by

Joyce Kirby

Published by

Hampsthwaite Village Society

©

Hampsthwaite Village Society

ISBN:

0-9533723-0-8

Published 1999

All rights reserved. No part of
this publication may be reproduced
in any form or by any means
without the prior permission
of the Hampsthwaite Village Society

Printed in Great Britain by
Kall Kwik Harrogate
Regent House, John Street
Harrogate, HG1 1JZ

CONTENTS

Foreword to the History
  of Hampsthwaite — Kate Bennison

Bygone Days — Annie Pawson

Well I remember..... — Monica Addyman

"Let me --- but keep a farm" — Edward Brown

Life in a Village Shop in
  the Thirties and Forties — Gladys Calvert

Reminiscences — Eric Lundell

"Of days that used to be" — Doreen Nelson

My Early Years and Life
  at Hampsthwaite School — Janet Pritchard

Remembrance of Things Past — Ralph Robinson

Memories are made of this — Winifred Steel

"I remember, I remember,
  the house where I was born " — George Wainwright

A Walk down Memory Lane — Bernard Wilson

Foreword to the

History of Hampsthwaite

It gives me great pleasure to introduce the first book in our series on the History of Hampsthwaite. Over the years several attempts have been made to write such a history, the first one twenty years ago. Some were serious, some more light-hearted, but all foundered.

In 1993 a small group of members of Hampsthwaite Village Society met to discuss this project and, as confidence grew, to write it. Our history will go backwards through time, starting with "Villagers' Reminiscences" - contributed by residents who have lived here for all or most of their lives. Book 2 will cover "Buildings and Their Stories", Book 3 "The Twentieth Century" and, finally, Book 4 "Early History from Roman Times".

We extend our grateful thanks to all those who have helped in any way: to Dr. Ian Richardson for his initial advice on the early history and on essential research; to Mrs. P.D. Walker of Walkers in Oxford Street, Harrogate for her guidance through the intricacies of publishing and her invaluable support; to Mr. George Capel of Harrogate Reference Library and Mr. Malcolm Neesam for their wise advice; to Mr. Ian Haden for his photographic expertise, his meticulous care in preparing the prints and his unstinting gift of time; to Mr. Mozi Nami for his skill in preparing our disc file, his tireless efforts in tracking down printers and his unbounded enthusiasm, which kept our spirits high - even in times of major crisis; to the many who have provided archive material. But, of course, none of this would have been possible without the dedicated, hard work of our editor, Joyce Kirby, who has had the onerous job of collating and proof-reading all the material.

I hope that our readers will enjoy our village history as much as we have enjoyed compiling it.

Kate Bennison
Chairman, Hampsthwaite
Village Society

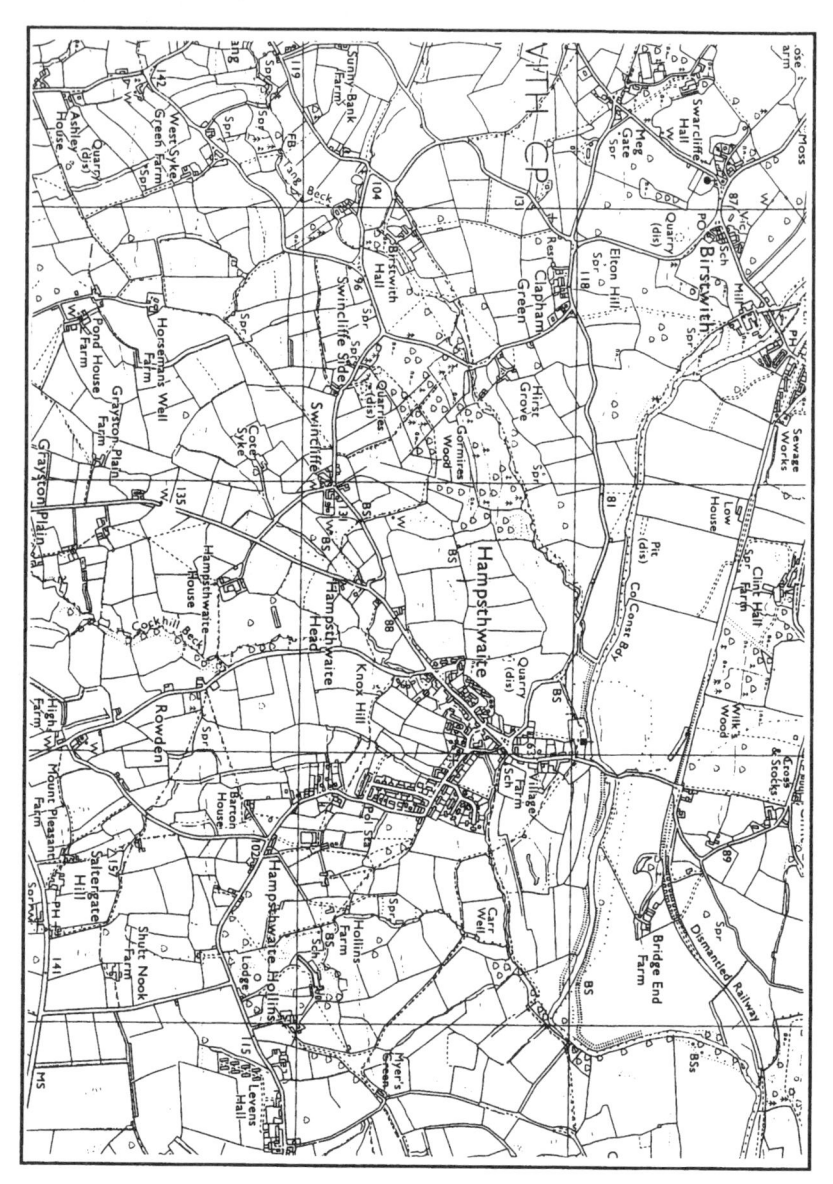

HAMPSTHWAITE AND ITS ENVIRONS

Reproduced from 1980 HARROGATE: Sheet SE25/35, Scale 1:25000 map by permission of Ordnance Survey on behalf of The Controller of Her Majesty's Stationery Office, c Crown Copyright Licence No. MC02783.

BYGONE DAYS:
the village of Hampsthwaite as it was at the turn of the century

ANNIE PAWSON
1901-1991

BYGONE DAYS:
the village of Hampsthwaite as it was at the turn of the century

ANNIE PAWSON

The following account is taken from a conversation between Mary Johnson and Annie Pawson recorded in September 1981. In it Annie talks of her memories of the village when she was a girl.

The Village

Hampsthwaite was just one long street when I was young - Hollins and the Closes had not been built. I can recall twenty-two thatched cottages, thatched farmhouses and a thatched blacksmith's "shop" as we called it - the smithy, you know. As for the shops, well, the roads are much wider now, but then at the junction of Hollins Lane with the High Street - opposite the present corner shop - was the old Post Office, from which they sent messages by Morse code, and over the road from Mr. Lundell's (Ivy Cottage) was a general store with cottages at the side.

I used to come down with my aunt from my grandma's right up Grayston Plain to shop at the general store. While auntie was being served, I went through to the old gentleman at the back and sat on his lap. Meanwhile his wife, who had an old lace cap and apron typical of the time, was weighing everything on the old-fashioned brass scales and was making bags for the currants, sugar and other groceries. Auntie always bought six pennyworth of yeast, because everyone had to bake - there was no bread for sale in the village then. Another regular purchase was a quarter of mint imperials - "white alberts" we called them - for grandma. When I heard the old lady rattling the sweets out of the big glass jar into the paper-bag, I slipped off her husband's knee in the hope that she would drop one on the floor, but she never did, even though she was very shaky!

At the top of the village was another shop, owned by Mr. Metcalfe and his wife, who was my grandma's friend, they having gone to school together. The building was very old with big rafters - and treacle and vinegar had to be tapped from barrels. When Mr. Metcalfe wanted to serve bacon, he would take down a side, cut out a big square and slice it with a carving knife. Then, if his customer wanted tobacco twist, he would take the same knife, wipe it on his apron and use it to cut the "baccy", which he measured by the spindle of his wrist. He had lots of little drawers, which held cloves and old spices. He had wonderful cardboard posters, depicting young ladies wearing boaters and dresses with leg-of-mutton sleeves and long skirts: they were advertising Mother Seigel's syrup and Mazarati tea. The Metcalfe's kept everything: tape, buttons, flannelette for shirts, wool for knitting stockings.

There was one butcher - a right high trap he had - who went to all the outlying districts. His was all fresh meat, so it was much dearer than that in Harrogate.

I don't remember, but mother did, that down at "Cornerstone" opposite the church was the Lamb Inn. The publican did not know that his little girls were in the Band of Hope (of which more later), until one month he happened to look out of the window as the procession approached and there were his daughters carrying the banner! It gave him such a shock - not to mention food for thought. Ten days later he took the Lamb Inn sign down and put it

The Lamb Inn, which later became the Temperance Hotel

over the bridge wall into the river, became an abstainer and called the inn "The Temperance Hotel", a name which it kept until comparatively recently. The old seats stood around, raised up from the flags, padded to the walls like they used to be in public houses.

There was only the school building for the main village events like dances and concerts. Of course, there was also the Village Room, donated by charity.

The Village Room

The men went there to read their daily papers and to play dominoes. Monday evening was "penny reading night", when we paid a penny to hear someone reading or playing the accordion. The young men would entertain as well and give a reading from a book or an old magazine. It was a happy evening, the highlight of the week.

Before the Scar reservoir was built, the river used to come rushing down to half way up the railway bank. Sometimes it even reached the fields down by the woods on the Lings and parts of the churchyard. Hen houses, sheep and all sorts of debris came down with the floods and ended up in the woods, where they lay rotting. People cleared their own fields, but did not accept responsibility for the woodland area.

The beck was important. Every so far there were steps down to it, because it had to be used for general household purposes ~ for washing up and washing clothes, for example, everyone went down with buckets to collect the water. Hollows were dug out to make water collection easier. Pump-water had to be preserved for drinking.

By the way, the Cockhill Beck was not always so-called. In grandma's day there used to be cock fights "up Rowden down Dicky Banks". There was a sort of amphitheatre there with a big, flat piece at the bottom. That was where the illegal cock fights were held - out of sight. The beck flowed right past that spot and that was how it got its name "Cockhill".

Thinking of water, grandma's supply had to come from the bottom of the hill. Auntie used to carry it: she had wooden yokes and two pails, one on each side, which she dipped into a square well at the edge of the road. Believe it or not, it is still there by Florence House, but it is overgrown with thorn bushes now.

After lunch at school and before afternoon lessons, we went to fetch water from the well or from one of the three pumps: there was one on the Green, one in the yard where Mr. Horner lives and one at the top of the village. I caught typhoid from that one. Little worms used to come through it with the water and, when that happened, the water had to be poured away. It transpired that the water ran down from the farms and that that was what caused the disease.

The pump on the Village Green

When the water level sank, the wells had to be primed with any water that could be found in order to make the supply flow again. In times of shortage the cows had to be taken from the farms to the river to drink. We even walked them on Birstwith Lane to a little patch there. They were very hard times for everyone.

The roads were very rough. When I grew older I always wore clogs to come down to the village, because there was puddle in winter, thick dust in summer. You see, the roads were repaired with stone from the local quarry at Clint. There was a high footpath there and the road was so narrow that, if there were a horse and cart with a load at the top, a whistle would be blown in warning so that anyone about to set off from the bottom would wait. The stones were left at the side of the road in heaps by "stone-breakers", who had sacks tied around their knees and who wielded long hammers to tap the stones. They were paid 2/6 per load of nut-sized pieces. This was the only means of road-repair.

Down in the village all the paths were paved with cobbles collected from the river-bed - there are still some of them lying under the tarmac. Those cobbles had to be weeded twice a year, once being in July for the Hampsthwaite Feast. We had to get down on our knees with a mat and an old fork to poke out the grass. We wouldn't have dared to do otherwise.

The Family

I had happy days at Grandma and Grandpa's. Their house was ever so low. All the floors had old stone flags and in the living room Grandpa had had to remove one of the flags to make a resting place for the grandfather clock, which otherwise would have been too tall for the room. All the buildings were low in those days; in fact, many of the cottages were only one storey high. But I digress. Access to Grandma's bedroom was by way of stone steps without a handrail; access to the second bedroom was through Grandma's. The door lintels, both downstairs and up, were made of thick stone and all the doors, including that of the parlour, had finger-holes through which one lifted the latch. I used to say to Grandma, "Can I open the 'parsley' door?". I loved to look in the parlour - it was really old-fashioned, with its antimacassars and a little three-legged table, covered with a crocheted cloth on which the family Bible sat. In the kitchen was a very old fireplace with black-leaded ovens and a stone-flagged pit in the hearth, into which the ashes dropped. Any cinders were used again. Once I was rocking in a little chair and I rocked too near the fire. The result? - a scorched chin! Light was provided by paraffin lamps and candles, some of tallow and some of wax.

Grandpa had a threshing machine and, when it was taken out on the road, he rode on horseback in front of it, with a red flag to warn everyone that it was coming along. He was also an inventor and, when he lost an arm in an accident, made himself an artificial one with a hook at the end, then adapted his tools so that they would fit into this. I was fascinated by his inventions, the brain-children of a man who could neither read nor write. He had never gone to school because he was considered to be too delicate.

Every morning we were expected to do farm chores: we had to feed the chickens, put the turnips in the chopper for the farm manager, break up the cow cake with a hammer, do the milking. Well, I should have helped with the milking, but it defeated me - I just did not have the grip in my wrists. Sometimes on the radio they ask what sounds listeners would like to hear. I loved the farm sounds: I loved the clatter and rattle of the galvanised buckets as the milkers put them down; I loved to wake up to the cock crowing and the hens prating - there were no battery hens then. They were happy days.

My great aunt lived in one of the two cottages next to the old stable. She had left the farm when her husband died and had one son, who eventually went to Australia, where he became a professor. Sadly, she did not hear from him for years, but she used to save money for him and have it posted off by the schoolmaster. She had arranged for one of mother's brothers to manage the farm before he was thirteen years old. In winter she expected him to knit socks or make pricked rugs, which she sold; in summer he had to gather brambles and other fruits so that she could make jams and wines to sell. Every Thursday he took her to the train for Harrogate with her butter baskets of goodies for sale. He never liked the farm, which is not surprising when you realise that he was paid only £5 for two years' work!

The house "up Hollins" where mother was born was haunted. It was known as "the boggart house" by everyone. Grandpa never allowed the girls to sleep in a particular bedroom, which had red stains, which no one succeeded in planing out. It was always said that a lady had been beheaded there and that she was heard, but never seen. Actually, people were frightened when they had no cause to be.

Thinking of "hauntings", there were some old elms down near the well trough that shone silvery white in the moonlight. We had to stand on tiptoe to look down into it and that was haunted too. One night a man was so frightened that he would not go past and he told Grandpa that the boggart was at the well. Grandpa went to look and found that one of the elms had blown down. In the space where it had been uprooted there were two fluorescent eyes as big as saucers!

And still on the subject of "hauntings", Grandma once described how, on her way down to the village one evening, a black dog came across the road in front of her and vanished in the middle of it. She never did find an explanation for that.

The School

When I went to the Village School there were about ninety-six pupils. We sat at old-fashioned desks with iron frames. There were no exercise books, pencils or pens - just slates and slate pencils, which squeaked when they needed to be sharpened. As infants, we had sand trays in which we wrote our letters and did simple drawings. We were not allowed to touch them between lessons; the teacher shook them so that the sand did not all collect in one corner.

The boys wore clogs or very heavy hob-nailed boots, corduroy suits - jackets and trousers which came just below the knee - and celluloid collars; we girls had buttoned-up or laced boots and, my goodness, it was difficult once one lost the tags to get them through the holes. My great uncle, my grandmother's brother, was a cobbler and shoemaker in the village, so he always made my boots, which I had to continue to wear even when they became too tight, because they were so expensive. When I grew older and we went up to a farm on the Skipton Road, I wore clogs in the winter because we had to walk all the way down to school, setting off before eight o' clock in the morning.

As the Village School was C. of E. and Church and School were very closely linked, the Vicar was much in evidence. At five to nine the school bell tolled a warning; at nine o'clock it was rung again and that was it! Anyone late was caned. The Vicar took Assembly: we sang a hymn and said prayers. That was followed by three quarters of an hour's Religious Instruction - he would read the Bible and explain it to us. Otherwise, most of the time was spent on the three R's. I never liked music: I felt that I "couldn't sing right", which was rather unfortunate as the teacher was a trained singer. I said before that we had slates and slate pencils, but when we were older we did progress to pens and inkwells. The boys used to mix the powder and water in the porch. If pens were dropped on the floor the nibs became crossed, so we constantly needed new ones - and woe betide us if we didn't use them properly: we had to go thin on the up-stroke and press thick on the down-stroke.

Naturally, the schoolmaster taught us, whilst his wife instructed the Infants in the three R's and the older girls in housewifery and sewing <u>and</u> darning of socks or patching of clothes once a week. We even learned the theory of cooking, but never practised it! Yes, you could say that we had a smattering of all the rudimentary skills. The top class was called the 6+ Standard and we stayed in it until we left school at thirteen. There was no 11+ examination then - nor were there school dinners. We took our Lunch in black leather satchels, made by "Saddler" Haxby, and went to the house of two maiden ladies, who charged a halfpenny a mug for very weak tea, made from scalded tea-leaves. One of the ladies would pour it out and sweeten it, stirring it with a little old yellow spoon. So that we should not know how meagre an amount of sugar she was giving us, she would distract us by reciting silly poetry:

> Little Willie
> was so silly he tumbled over a cinder;
> he bent his bow
> and shot a crow
> and killed a cat in 'winder' (= window)

This same lady made bee wine, but I never saw the bees. It stood in 2lb glass jam jars all the way along the windowsill. It was some sort of fungus, you know.

We used to play merils, a rustic game played by two persons with counters, on a flat stone on which a figure was marked, consisting of three squares one within another; the object was to get three counters in a row at the intersection of the lines joining the corners and the mid-points of the sides. Up at Swincliffe there was a natural round stone at ground level. It had holes in it and we used that. Rumour had it that an old archer, a very strong man who lived at the Bay Horse, once stood on that stone, stretched his bow with his hands and feet and shot an arrow right to Clint!

Going down to school it was fun: we all took our hoops - wooden ones for the girls, iron ones for the boys. As we bowled them along, we hummed and sang. Sometimes they ran out of control, crashed into a wall and split. Then they had to be taken to the blacksmith's to be repaired. It cost 2d to have one welded. Worst of all were the walks back up the hill from school in the summer, when it was so hot - particularly as we were expected to be home by five o'clock. If we were late, we were in real trouble, because there were so many chores to do before we could have our evening meal.

After leaving school most of the girls went into domestic service - locally at somewhere like the vicarage at first, then, as they became more skilled, further away; the boys became labourers on the farms. It was a great day when Dorothy Barker went to Ripon to train as a teacher. The schoolmaster's daughter had coached her in the evenings for this. She is the only one that I can remember who reached such dizzy heights.

Yorkshire Penny Bank

There was a bank, a Yorkshire Penny Bank, in the Village School on Friday evenings. The adults used it after classes finished, because it was the only one locally. We had to come all the way down from the Skipton Road Farm when we wanted to pay in any money.

Church

Because the Village School was C. of E. and, as I said before, the Vicar was much in evidence, we all had to go to church.

*A member of Hampsthwaite Parish Church, Annie
received the Maundy Money from HM Queen Elizabeth II
at Ripon Cathedral on 4th April, 1985*

The Vicar's wife took a morning Sunday School at half past nine in the day school. If there were any missionary meetings, I was expected to recite. That was no punishment as I loved poetry. We also had to dance around the maypole at the Garden Fete held in the Vicarage grounds annually. We wore white voile dresses for such occasions and looked really smart - and we never went to church without hats, lovely straw hats with daisies and buttercups around them. We were pretty girls. Now, it is hard to distinguish boys from girls when they all dress alike.

In my young days people only went to funerals if they were "bidden". The undertaker would ask the bereaved family who was to be invited, then would pay a man half-a-crown to go around "bidding". He would say, "You are bidden to ------ 's funeral on such and such a day at such and such a time. Please be present". As the time of the funeral approached, the church bell would be tolled. We could hear it right up at the top farm and, as it tolled, we counted: three ones for a child, three threes for a woman, three sixes for a man. The funeral tea after the service was always held at the Temperance Hotel. The lady there would ask the mourners in advance whether they wanted it with ham or potted meat sandwiches.

When Turner Grainge, the Wesleyan Minister, died in 1911 at the age of ninety-six, all the children had to process two by two to the funeral service. He was quite a character, living across the Green and always wearing a plaid shawl. He kept the records for the church down here for years at an annual payment of half-a-crown.

Chapel

When the new Chapel was built, I went to the opening with Grandpa. Then, in the following June, I attended the first Flower Service, taking forget-me-nots and pansies, which I had begged from some nieces of Grandma. A little three-year-old, Emma Barker, was sitting in front of me at the service and at one point she sang "Land and Sea" to her mother's accompaniment.

Transport

In my childhood there were no cars - only horses and traps. We were told never to throw any paper about outside because, if we did and the wind blew it, it could cause a horse to shy and bolt. At one Hampsthwaite Feast, the postman was coming around Birstwith corner in his trap, when the horse bolted at the Fair entrance. A man who tried to stop it was dragged along and killed. Grandpa had a trap too and, when we were tiny, he sometimes took us into Harrogate as a treat.

There was not much transport into town - only a train in the morning at eight o'clock. A solicitor travelled on this and my sister, who was a stenographer. Two years ago, I gave the Railway Museum in York her last pass to Harrogate. Would you believe that it cost just over £1 for three months? Because fares were cheap, as we got older we went on a summer trip to Redcar. Starting from Pateley, the train picked up trippers all the way down the line and we had a wonderful day at the seaside.

Annual holidays were unknown, but one highlight of the year was the Sunday School Treat, when we had a flat cart - a coal cart swept clean - drawn by a horse and with two long forms back to back. We went far into the country with our buns and brown paper flour bags to "scramble nuts". I remember one boy who refused to join in any of the games. Eventually he was dragged into the circle and, as he jigged around, buns began to fall out from under his blouse. He was severely reprimanded for "stealing", when what had really happened was that he had promised to take the buns back to his younger brothers and sisters and to forgo his own enjoyment. I did weep for him.

"Shank's Pony"

We had to walk the four and a quarter miles to town to school when we were older and to the fishmonger's every Good Friday. Sometimes we went in at night, but it was so very dark as we came home. We would look back at the lights to console ourselves and would do the journey in stages - down to the gasworks, then to the blacksmith's shop at the Traveller's Rest and finally home.

The village women walked into Harrogate on Saturdays when there was no train. Each carried two carpet bags and a zinc bucket. They always bought cheap Argentinian meat, which went runny when it thawed, so it had to be carried home in the buckets.

A Mr. Forrest, who worked on the reservoirs, covered many miles as he walked to and from work. He would set off for home on a Friday evening and would arrive in the middle of the night. By Sunday afternoon he would be on his way back to the reservoirs again to re-start work on the Monday.

As there were no trucks to transport the animals, the cowherds would drive the cows to the auctions at Pannal and Otley. Even geese had to be driven to the fairs.

Village Entertainment

The menfolk frequently got drunk - it was the hops, I suppose. On Friday nights those who worked up at the quarry at Swincliffe Top were paid; on Saturdays they went to the Joiner's Arms, imbibed too much and fought. There was one who became jolly, rolled on the road just like a puppy, sang and gave the kiddies halfpennies.

I mentioned before that the Village School had to be used for the main social events. When a dance was going to be held, because the floor was old and rough, soap powder was sprinkled on it to make it slippery. After the dance was over, some volunteers had to stay up until about four o'clock in the morning to scrub it ready for school that day. They don't have to do things like that now, do they?

The Hampsthwaite Feast used to be on Cross Green (the Village Green). There was a fairground with roundabouts, a coconut-shy, an Aunt Sally (at which sticks or balls were thrown to smash a pipe in the mouth of a wooden figure), stalls selling brandy snaps, fruit, toys - the favourites being little wooden horses on four iron wheels, with a stick attached to push them - and hobby horses. The stalls were sited where the telephone box is now and down the main street going towards the school. There wasn't the traffic that there is now, so the festivities did not cause any problems. There were even pony races and donkey races on Birstwith Lane. Competitions were held up the steps in the Joiner's Arms' yard, where there was always a prize for the man who could pull the ugliest face through a horse collar: it was called "The face through the Barkhan".

Lots of Grandpa's relations came to stay for the Feast, so I had to sleep on a cured sheepskin on the floor by the tallboy, which to me seemed as tall as a giant. At mealtimes I had to eat in the dairy because there was no room at the table.

At Christmas time the mummers came to Grandma's. I was rather nervous when they arrived at two or three o'clock in the morning and called out, "Good morning, Mr. Phillips; nice, bright morning", then recited a rhyme. When Grandma and Grandpa came downstairs to light the fire, I crept down to join them. The mummers, with faces blacked, were given cake and wine. Once one of them pulled an orange out of his pocket to tempt me. I was scared stiff. They wore straw boaters and multi-coloured clothes. One had a banjo and another a concertina. After they went away I had nightmares and my Grandma took me into her bed to comfort me.

Pedlars often came around with their wares. One man from Harrogate brought a butter basket full of pikelets and crumpets.

Another pushed a hurdy-gurdy all the way from town. Whenever he arrived, two old ladies in the village gave him sixpence apiece to play dance music while, dressed in clean aprons, they waltzed to the tunes up by Metcalfe's shop.

Village Characters

Canon Peck - he was a "Reverend" at first - did a great deal for Hampsthwaite Church. He was a good vicar, like a father to everyone, knowing each parishioner from the cradle to the grave. When he met an adult outside, he always enquired about the offspring's progress at school. If he encountered me in the village he asked, "How's your Grandma?" Secreted in his pocket were a bottle of Parrish's Food and one of emulsion to "doctor" those who could not afford medical fees.

There was a resident doctor in the village, Dr. Ashby, who died in 1913. My brother, born in 1912, was the last baby that he brought into the world. He lived at Thimbleby House, where the Bowen's are now (i.e. in 1981 - followed by the Faber's and then the Hudson's), for years and years. He had a family born to him there. The house had a very wide back door and, if anyone went for medicine at night, the housekeeper would answer the door, ask what was wanted and pass the packet through a plate-sized hole in the door, which had a shutter that swivelled round. There were no free prescriptions then and the doctor would do little operations himself. He was marvellous.

Mrs. Wright at Hollins Hall was a great "abstinence" lady. An ardent teetotaller, she always said that, when she was on her death-bed, she was not to be given brandy or other intoxicating liquor. She had us once a week for a Band of Hope meeting, at which we sang "Land of Hope" and "Water Bright", but the highlight was a mug of milk and a bun! Once a month the boys and girls, wearing straw boaters with blue ribbons and led by a beautiful sky-blue banner with "Hampsthwaite Band of Hope" printed on it in gold letters, were marched down to the church. Mrs. Wright was a very good church worker who, in my mother's time, had her head gardener plant two hundred small daffodil bulbs in the churchyard. She chose the low-growing variety so that the wind would not snap them off. Unfortunately, although the sheep do a good job in keeping the churchyard tidy, they must also be held responsible for the gradual decline in the numbers of daffodils over the years. After the last war, I planted the crocuses and daffodils around the war memorial.

In our schooldays the remains of Thackeray's cottage was a joiner's shop. "Saddler" Haxby was the last to own the property. He was the oldest saddler in Yorkshire and, I think I'm right in saying, the third oldest in the whole of England. When we came down to school, we often had to carry a horse collar for him to repair.

At the cottage next to "Thompson's Garth", Mrs. Pidgeon's

Mally's Cottage

home, lived an old lady called Mally. She was not a witch, but she could foresee the future to a certain extent. She washed for Grandma. Someone once did what Grandpa called "a mucky trick" up at the farm. What exactly happened I don't know, but he wanted to discover who was responsible. Mally told him to take a handful of hay, two handfuls of salt and a big bunch of holly and to use them to make a fire. She was adamant that the guilty party would come to the door in flames. Grandpa did not dare to follow her instructions in case someone really did appear!

World Wars

During World War I there was a camp of tents and mules in the village. In World War II soldiers were billeted in the Village Room and a bridge was built across the beck to the toilets beyond. One soldier - he was no more than eighteen years old - reported sick to the M.O. with a very bad attack of influenza. Later he had to have some teeth extracted at the dentist's, developed depression and committed suicide. He was buried in Hampsthwaite churchyard without any family present. I used to take flowers to the grave in his remembrance. I just felt very sad that such a young fellow should have died in that way: he had needed understanding, but no one had been prepared to give it.

Past and Present

For the most part there were very few social distinctions in the village, although I can think of one vicar who always insisted that everyone should bow to him and, of course, if we met Mrs. Wright from Hollins Hall in the street, we girls dropped a curtsey, whilst the boys touched their caps.

Poverty was a problem. I think sometimes of all the roast beef I gave away as a girl on my way to school. There was one family of twelve children and, my goodness, they were poor, the poorest people I have ever known. The mother was caretaker for a little mission and many was the time she walked half a mile, paraffin lamp in hand, for the preacher. Her husband, a keeper up Beckwithshaw way for Ripley Castle, was really smart with his polished-up leggings and waxed moustache, but the children never had shoes on their feet - and Maggie, one of the little ones, had nothing to wear except an old lady's chemise until the day she started school.

One night, one of the girls came to ask if I might go to sit with her, as her mother was going out. Some time later, as we sat together, there was whining from some of the little ones upstairs. I will never forget what I saw when we went up to them. There were only two little bedrooms for the parents and twelve children and they had mattresses on the floor, head to toe for the smaller ones, with two children at one end and two at the other. Although it was winter, they had only one cover, a thin blanket, over which they were quarrelling as each pulled it. Do you know, even if the mattress had had no one lying on it, that blanket would scarcely have stretched across. The girl knew how to cope with them. She whipped it off, smacked each bare behind and put it back on again! They did not say another word. Even now, in winter when it is very cold, the picture of those children comes before my eyes.

When they came to school, we met them part way down the road at a stile. They all had dripping and bread with bits of salt on it, or sometimes a scraping of lard. That was <u>their</u> lunch. Meanwhile <u>we</u> had slices of beef in bread and butter, homemade teacakes, buttered shortcakes - a plain and a currant one - and a slice of jam pasty. We were tired of cold roast beef, so, when we met them, we exchanged our sandwiches for their dripping and bread.

The oldest five were girls and, as each reached thirteen, went into domestic service on one of the farms; the boys in their turn did farm-labouring.

Close by our farm there were four or five old cottages for farm-labourers. If they thought that there was any baking going on at the farm, two little boys from there would appear and Auntie would give them bread. Once, just before Christmas, they knocked at the door and she gave them each a mince pie, hot from the oven. A minute later there was another knock. Said one, "Please can he have a teaspoon to scrape the muck out of his pie?". He had never seen mincemeat in his life.

Doctors, as I explained before, had always to be paid in those days. There was no National Health Service so, in case of illness, one helped if one could, because the poor found it difficult to pay for medication. One doctor was very kind: he sent his bills out, but he never pressed for payment.

Because wages were so low, it was up to each individual to try to plan for "the rainy day". Otherwise, anyone who fell ill and could no longer work had to go to the workhouse. Each family was also expected to take responsibility for aging parents. If an elderly father could not work and no one member of the family could provide for him and the mother, then all the sons had to give a few shillings a week to allow them to stay in their own home. People nowadays do not know what real poverty is.

The village used to be a closely-knit community, with everyone knowing everyone else. Why, until about fifteen years ago I could have told you the name of every person in the area. Now it has grown too large. I just do not approve of all these incomers.

In the past everyone worked hard and appreciated the little leisure time available. Now they do not know that they are born and they are always grumbling. Life is too easy. Hard work produces a good citizen. What one wants one has to strive to achieve and not have it handed to one on a plate.

I know that one cannot put the clock back. I enjoy my present life and I remember the past with affection. The future I view with some trepidation because of failing health. We have lost much of the milk of human kindness, but there are still good people around, quietly going about their business and ever ready to offer a helping hand. We hear little of them because the good do not make news, only the bad.

When I was with Grandpa, I had a little stool ~ I still have it now - and I had to be seen and not heard. At night farmers came to talk about their crops - that was how all the information was passed on. They never mentioned dates, only incidents: they would say, "It happened when mare went mad" or "It was when cow tumbled in well" - much more graphic than pin-pointing a year. Now everything takes second place to T.V. - the art of conversation is a thing of the past.

It was a grand life but, as I have shown, there was poverty and destitution. Thank God, that is not the case now, for materially - speaking life is much, much easier. I doubt, however, whether folk are happier, even though some of them think that I was brought up in the bad old days. From where I stand the present generation is too restless, is in too much of a hurry: it needs time to "stand and stare", to think before it acts.

WELL I REMEMBER

MONICA ADDYMAN

"WELL I REMEMBER ----"

MONICA ADDYMAN

The Family

Years ago one of my husband Fred's grandfathers, Jimmy Addyman, farmed in Hampsthwaite at Bridge End Farm. Later, in Fred's father Dearlove's time, <u>he</u> had someone living in to look after everything. When Mary Addyman (Mrs. Hornshaw), Fred's sister, was old enough, she went to live with the maternal grandparents on their farm, Shutt Nook - opposite the Nelson Arms - because they were on their own by then. On Sundays Fred himself would go in the horse and trap to see them and they would put him in their rarely-used parlour to have a nap. He said that it smelt really fusty. To return to Mary, she was the eldest sister in the Addyman family and the last to die. She, her husband and family farmed at Killinghall. Fred himself died in 1992, February 4th to be exact.

The Property

Fred's father rented Home Farm from the Greenwood family. It was later bought by Clifford Lister at the Swarcliffe sale in 1948. In the village, the area behind the school was included with our land - right up to Pinkney's house and down to Dearlove's Wood, from where there is still a walk to Killinghall. We have land at Starbeck too - backing on to the old General Hospital. That came with the Swarcliffe Estate, as too did Bridge End Farm, which - as I mentioned before - Fred's grandfather had always rented. The Abattoir was ours until Fred retired.

"The abattoir was ours until Fred retired"

    According to various builders, who have been in the house to do electrical work, "Ashville" started life as a simple two-up, two-down cottage. Strangely, on the house deeds - kept safely by the solicitor - are the names of many of the past vicars of St. Thomas à Becket Church. (Research is currently taking place to establish the significance of this list and a note will be appended at a later date).

The back of Ashville

Butchering

We used to supply meat to our own businesses in Leeds. In fact, three shops in the city still have our name up. We also delivered to all the big butchers in Harrogate. Addyman's was the only butcher's around here. The drivers, amongst whom was Jimmy Hammond, had to change horses when they went up the Dale, because they would spend several days delivering, going right up beyond Swarcliffe. It was a slow job then. We have nothing to do with butchering any more, because the whole family has died out.

Courtship and Marriage

My sister was married just before the war. She and her husband went to live in a cottage in Lund Lane when he returned from active service in 1946. Fred and my brother-in-law had met up at dances which they both attended and that was how I first saw my husband-to-be.

In our courting days I lived at Bramhope. It was during wartime petrol rationing, which made life difficult. It was also a time when there was heavy bombing over Leeds and we lived near the aerodrome, a dicey situation.

We married in late 1942, over fifty years ago. It was a marriage which almost didn't happen! The taxi-driver forgot to come for my father and me. All the neighbourhood children were waiting outside for us to depart and eventually the photographer came to our rescue. Father sat in the front beside him, whilst I squeezed into the back "dickey seat" with all the paraphernalia. I can laugh about it now, but it was very worrying at the time. As the service started, neither Fred nor I could concentrate. He kept saying to me, "Where have you been?" Our organist was rather special: he

"We married in late 1942"

had played for all the big dances in Ilkley. As you can imagine, he had filled the gap before my arrival with some lovely music.

I forgot to mention that there was a sadness over the occasion, because Fred's sister, Sophia, had died only a fortnight before our big day.

And so to Hampsthwaite

Previously, Fred had lived at New Park, above the butcher's shop there, but he knew a lot about the village. For me it was a big change to come to sleepy Hampsthwaite. I had always been taught to make myself useful, but it really was rough coming here - and cold, so cold. Of course, there was no central heating, only what was called a "side oven". It was heated by a fire, kept on all night, stacked up with slack (coal dust) to "keep it in", so that it was still burning in the morning, guaranteeing plenty of hot water.

Next to the living room/kitchen was a small area with a sloping roof, where there were slabs for bacon, hams and the rest, which we had cured. I knew all about curing - I must have dealt with tons of bacon. You see, my father was very useful and had explained the process to me. He was an expert cook and made all his offspring's wedding cakes. His skill rubbed off on me, the youngest of a family of three: my siblings were an elder brother, now dead, and a sister.

In the bedrooms we had brass electric lights, to which string was attached for use during the night - you know! I think that army personnel must have been billeted in the house, because there were dart holes in all the doors, which had to be replaced. They were such a mess, oh dear, they were.

Employees

Our labourers in the early forties included German, Polish and Italian prisoners of war. They were brought from a camp near Ripon and dropped off daily at the various farms - the answer to the man-power shortage, caused when all those sound of limb were called up for military service. It was really unbelievable the hours that they worked to keep a food supply going.

At meal-times I used a huge table, fully extended. There would be perhaps two German prisoners and all the Houseman family - including Bernard, who lived up at Brimham Rocks Farm - and Mrs. Penrose, who eventually came to live in one of the cottages, later demolished, down by the church. I cooked for them and waited on them. When they were "doing the corn", they worked from dawn to dusk. It was so dusty then - I took drinks down to the fields at night. They were hard times, but that was the accepted way of life then.

Fred employed several of the village boys and it used to be a real pantomime with them all. They were constantly falling out, but they "fell in" again! They never did anything really bad, not like today. My husband used to smooth things over - he was a kind employer, who appreciated how hard they worked.

Lambing time 1953

We kept cattle, sheep, pigs - the lot. And there was a great big boiler - where the late Mr. Bill Allen's bungalow stands today - which one of the boys oversaw in the evenings.

Fred with his prize bull

Thinking of the Past

Fred used to tell me how people came from the surrounding villages and walked down Church Street to the station to catch the train to Scarborough. It was easier to travel to the coast by public transport then than now, when people without cars are stuck.

Our menfolk went to all the auctions. If anyone missed a session, the others passed on all the news to him. A favourite meeting place for the farmers from Otley was the Temperance Hotel, originally called the Lamb Inn.

The famous day of the flood in July 1968, I was frantically trying to block up the front of the house, while firemen were pumping out the cellar - under which even now there is a well. And

The front of Ashville

there was still an old pump in the living room when I came here. But I digress. The well was found by workmen, who were encouraged by my husband to go on digging in the hope of coming upon some treasure trove! Needless to say, they were unsuccessful, so filled it in again. When Mr. Gordon Bailey moved to Thimbleby House across the road, he had pumps installed in his cellar to cope with emergencies.

I look back at these moments and they seem so long ago.

Pets et al.

While we had two dogs the cats never came inside. They stayed out in the barns and scavenged in the food bins for scraps from the hotels. Then the Cat Protection League persuaded me to adopt four cats as pets. Before I took them in, their little faces used to come over the railing, looking at me because they were hungry. Of course, I fed them and, having once done so, I continued. They are little dears. One of them is a real scavenger - she catches rabbits.

I dare not put nesting-boxes out now because of the cats. Thinking of our feathered friends, the river used to be a wonderful spot: I often saw cranes down there. My husband was never a fisherman, but we had fishing rights and used to stock our stretch of the river each year with trout. Some of the butchers used to come to tickle them, as too did the villagers. I believe that nowadays several of the young boys are allowed to have tickets, which authorise them to fish. A nice hobby.

Across at Bridge End there was a snicket leading down to the river. Strange to say, in days gone by, with all that water so near, the people who lived in the cottage in Ripley Wood had to go to Bridge End House for water, because they did not have any laid on in their own house. And mentioning Ripley Wood, which is so beautiful in bluebell time, it belongs to the Ripley Estate. We used to walk that way to the Ripley Show.

Afterthought

Reminiscing like this has made me realise how the years have flashed past - inevitable, I suppose, when one has always kept oneself busy.

Gone are the peaceful days before traffic used Church Lane as a race-track in the early evening; gone is the small, close-knit community of the past - all this the result of the growth of the village, which has become very much a dormitory for those who work in the nearby towns and cities. Alack-a-day!

"LET ME ……. BUT KEEP A FARM"

J. EDWARD BROWN

"LET ME .... BUT KEEP A FARM"

J. EDWARD BROWN

My maternal grandfather, Charles Ferdinand Vero, came to Cote Syke from Riva Hill Farm near Brimham Rocks in 1929 and there, reluctantly, Father joined him. Why reluctantly? Well, my father was one of three children born at Dringhouses, where his parents ran the Post Office, and eventually he found himself at Hartwith, near Brimham Rocks. There he met and wed my mother in 1926 and they made their home at Park House, Bishop Thornton, where they settled happily. It was a wrench to make the move down into Hampsthwaite, where incidentally his sister also came to live after she married Harry Grant.

There had been a big fire at Cote Syke in 1928 and the Aykroyds had bought it at that point. They renovated it before the

Cote Syke: built in 1702

arrival of my parents and grandparents the following year. It was regarded as very modern at the time with its bathroom and indoor toilet, luxuries which not many farmhouses in this area had, so far as I remember, until the fifties. At Cote Syke itself electricity did not arrive until 1953, later than mains water, which reached us in the mid-forties. Previously, we had been dependent upon five wells for our supply and problems arose when they ran dry. I can recall a time when my father went down to the Nidd with 17-gallon milk churns to provide us with water. On his return, he dipped one churn into the vat and a cow sauntered along and drank the lot, so he felt that he was on a never-ending conveyor belt!

I am an only child. I was born to my mother on Boxing Day 1930 after a hard labour. The doctor was in attendance right through Christmas Day and the following night. That seemed to put an end to any thought of enlarging the family. One like me was probably enough anyway!

I started school in 1935 at Hampsthwaite. Four years later, in 1939, the evacuees came to the village. The "London mothers" were the first that we had: there were two mothers and two boys, who lived in our sitting room. I don't know how on earth they managed. They did not stay very long and were followed by a boy from a farm school in Brighton. He was soon pinching things down in the village and was not at all popular as a result. His subsequent departure was a welcome relief. Eventually, a Mrs. Couchman arrived with her daughter. She had previously been at the Horner's at Manor Farm, but heard that we were "evacueeless" and asked us to take her in. She and Josie stayed for three and a half years and we are still friendly with Josie.

Mr. Couchman was an accountant in London and - to digress - after the war I benefited considerably from the family's friendship and kindness, spending a fortnight each year with them in the capital. Mr. Couchman took me to the great sporting venues - to

Lords and the Oval for cricket matches, to Wembley for football; Mrs. Couchman escorted me on conducted tours of the churches and abbeys. I had the best of both worlds and greatly appreciated my opportunities. Not many boys were so lucky.

To return to the war years, growing up on the farm was a happy time, but it seems so long ago now. I used to join the gang of six to eight boys on Grayston Plain at the corner and down to school we went. When I was given a bicycle, I used that as my transport.

In the 1940s a Young Farmers' Club was started, Father being one of the founders, and I joined when I was eleven. As well as making many friends there, I found it very educational from the agricultural point of view. As time went on, I became Press Secretary, then Treasurer and later Secretary for two or three years before being elected Chairman. Lastly, I became Club Leader. It was a great "marriage-making" organisation and probably still is. I met Kathleen there.

We married in 1955, after what Kathleen describes as "one of the longest courtships in the memory of the Young Farmers", and lived at Florence House - bought in 1954 - until in 1963 we moved down to Cote Syke, exchanging places with my parents. Before that little had altered after the initial renovations. I think that Mother had a new fireplace or two and that the Lounge and Kitchen were laid with red tiles - an improvement on the stone flags. When we arrived, we had the set-pot moved out of what is now a "Living Kitchen". Then, coal was stored in the coal-house at the back of the kitchen; oil heating was installed in the early seventies and what a difference that made. From being cold and draughty the rooms became snug and warm. Of course, we still kept the open fires, burning logs and coal - there is nothing quite like them.

Cote Syke has always been a happy house. In Mother and Father's day there was always someone calling. When speaking to

Mr. Frankland, who was born in the house in the late 1800s and who used to visit us, he confirmed what I am saying. That same atmosphere has continued from the nineteenth century to today, from the time of the Franklands to the present Browns.

The farm was Sir Frederic Aykroyd's showpiece and for many years, if he had visitors, he would bring them up unannounced to look around the house and the farm buildings - and to admire all that he had done. Eventually, he had the yard concreted and expected it to be kept swept. If he arrived and found that this had not been done, he would send a postcard to say that it had to be cleaned up before he came again. That also applied to thistles and fences: the former had to be cleared and the latter kept in a good state of repair. He was a good landlord.

I turn now to the gradual development of the farm. When the family settled into Cote Syke, the sale of milk was a first priority, as too was the making of butter until 1930. Milk for delivery in Harrogate was collected at the road end at 8 o'clock in the morning and at 3.30p.m. Later, when the Milk Board was established in 1933, it was taken into Leeds by Ralph Robinson in a small motor wagon.

I must break off for a moment to introduce you to my mother's Uncle Edward, who lived at Sunnyside Farm at Swincliffe Top. Mother did a lot of work for him because he was not very well - and he spent the last six months of his life in bed at Cote Syke. When my parents went out, I had to sleep with him in the big bed. I did that many times. If anyone called, we would blow out the candle and pretend that there was no one there!

While Uncle Edward was still at Sunnyside Farm, we would go up to visit him and Father would always smoke his pipe. Uncle would make me tell him not to burn his money - and I had to promise that I would never smoke when I grew up. He said that, if I kept my promise, he would leave me some cattle. I'm afraid I did break it once or twice and I had a guilty conscience about it. Notwithstanding, when he died he left me fourteen Aberdeen Angus cattle.

And now to revert to the farm. After Uncle's death in 1938, we did add a little more land to Cote Syke - about twenty acres - making a total of a hundred and twenty-eight in all. This made the farm somewhat larger than average, most being about forty acres. Time passed and in the mid-seventies we acquired about half of the Horners' farm - another forty acres. To this, in the late seventies we added half of Swincliffe Side Farm, when Mr. Allcock retired. The total by this time was two hundred acres and still, like Topsy, it "just growed". That was the general policy at the time.

So much for the land. On the production side we concentrated mainly on milk, gradually increasing our herd of cows. Our first milking machine arrived in 1936, a wonderful help. Until then, all the milking had been done by hand, at ten minutes per cow - a slow process. As a schoolboy, I was expected to milk one cow each morning before I set out for the village. I can remember her well: she was a three-teated white cow, a short-horn. We milked short-horns, like everyone else in the Dales, until TT testing began in the '40s. This was to eradicate TB, which had developed from drinking infected milk. As replacements we bought Ayrshire cattle, which came down from Scotland and, not long afterwards, changed again - this time to Friesians. It was in the '50s that we acquired our first pedigree British Friesians and now we have all-registered cattle.

But I digress again! When I left school in 1944 we had twenty cows, all kept inside from October until April, tied up by the neck. They even calved in that position and were never allowed to be loose at all. They were all fed by hand and cleaned out by hand - a big job. When they went out into the daylight in April, they appeared to be drunk as they staggered from side to side.

Meanwhile, we had converted another stable into a five-cow milking parlour - a 20% increase. From there we progressed to forty cows and then sixty.

It was not until the mid-60s that it became popular to "loose house" cattle. We had a big shed put up - 60' by 45'. It held sixty cows, which we brought out in batches of ten and led to the old cow-house, into which we had had a pipe-line installed. That eliminated all the carrying of milk, which went direct from the cow to the dairy.

In 1977 we put in power and modernised the parlour. We

Joseph in the modernised parlour

had cubicles fitted, one for each cow, and these were cleaned out by tractor. We also added a further parlour, which enabled ten cows - five each side - to be milked at once. That speeded things up for a time, until we increased the herd to make the procedure economical!

The sheep side of the farm is comparatively small. We used to "run" about forty ewes and now the number has increased considerably. We like the sheep because they keep the grass sweet and short and they clear the ragwort. Also, we think that they keep the sward in good balance. To graze only the cattle is not so satisfactory. We have some land up at the A59, about two miles away, which is set aside for the sheep. The lambs are sold at the local marts in Otley and Ripon. We also used Pannal in the past, but that market closed. To us sheep are a side-line - they don't make a vast profit, but they do "bring in a little bit".

Turning to the arable side of farming, I should explain first of all that, when I left school, we had already had to plough up quite an acreage of land to provide food - oats, barley, wheat, potatoes and turnips - for the cattle. This being wartime, we had also turned over five or six acres to potatoes for the locals. Originally, the actual planting of the seed-potatoes was done with the help of a horse-drawn plough, which produced a single furrow at a time, ready for the potatoes to be set by hand before being covered over; later the tractor came into its own.

At harvest time it was customary to employ school-children during the "tattie-scratting" holiday in October. There was competition amongst the farmers for their services and it was really a case of the one who paid the most - Listers, Phillips or one of several others amongst us - being successful. <u>We</u> usually took a gang of boys and girls gathered by Raymond Emmett, the "ganger" as we called him. To set the picking in motion, the horse and plough - or later the tractor with a potato spinner - would go down each furrow to loosen the soil and to dig out the newly-grown potatoes. However, because some of them remained covered over, they had to be scraped out by hand and foot - hence the phrase "tattie-scratting". The scratters brought their own lunch, but we provided the drinks - an important part of the procedure. They were happy times, particularly when the weather was fine.

The "tattie-scratters"

    The planting of the cereals - the "drilling" or sowing in rows in spring by horse and plough or tractor - led to the growing period, the ripening and thence to harvest when, cut with the binder, they were shaped into sheaves and "stooked" (= set up). Oat sheaves were stooked in sixes - three down either side; barley in threes or fours down either side; wheat in ten sheaves to the stook. The stooks were arranged in straight lines going up the field. If there were a bend in the line, there was trouble! This was because it was easier for the horse and cart or tractor to move up a straight row, as the stooks were forked on to the wagon for stacking. If it were fine weather, the oats and barley stayed in the field until the church bells had rung twice. The wheat did not need to stay out so long, because it dried more quickly and the sheaves were more open. I remember times when torrential downpours absolutely saturated the stooks, which began to sprout. Then we had to wait for a fine day before we could "twist" the inside of each sheaf out to help it to dry. It was very hard work and made one's fingers sore, especially if there were any thistles caught up in the stooks. And we certainly did not like to grow barley, because the "horns" went down our vests, a most uncomfortable sensation!

When the hired Marshall thrashing machine, owned by the Peacocks, arrived in the area, it usually stayed about a fortnight.

The Marshall thrasher

Ten or twelve farmers were needed to man it, so we all helped one another. Some men forked the sheaves from the stacks on to the thrasher. Then there was the bank cutter - and the feeder, but the corn-carriers - who, as their name suggests, carried the corn away after it was thrashed, were considered to have the plum job. As a boy, it was my task to do the chaff-carrying. If the machine broke down and ground to a halt, the chaff continued to come out. I could only hope for a windy day so that it would be blown away - the easiest way to dispose of it. Any that was saved was used for the animals' bedding.

For the farmers' wives too thrashing days were hard work. Between 7.30 am and 8.00 am they had to provide breakfast for the thrasher men, who arrived hungry on the doorstep. At ten o'clock they supplied "drinkings" for the many helpers, who by the middle of the day were pouring back inside for dinner, the set-pot being constantly in use and jam roly-poly being a favourite pudding. By mid-afternoon the wives were at the ready to produce "drinkings" a second time around. Moving from farm to farm as they did, the harvesters soon learned who were the good cooks and who were not! It was always a great help to have a wife who could produce a popular meal - there was no difficulty in finding helpers then.

But, to return to the harvesting for a moment - nowadays with the modern way of farming, the combine harvester does the job. For this reason barley is more often grown and the old oats have almost disappeared as a feed. Straw is baled in what we call "elephant toilet rolls"! The next step is square bales. As you can see, it has taken a long while and slow progress to "travel" from the 1940s to the 1990s.

Every farmer killed pigs. During the war this killing was restricted to two per household per year. The slaughter had to be carried out in the winter months, because all curing of bacon and ham had to be done in the cold weather. After they were salted to preserve them, they had to be hung, sometimes in a back bedroom, always in an airy place. The fatter the pigs, the more they were enjoyed. I have certainly eaten my share of the fat bacon and I do like a plate of home-cured ham.

My first recollection of a connection between our family and the church was because of Canon Peck, who prepared me for Confirmation when I was fourteen, along with about twelve other boys.

When Canon Peck retired in 1948, after fifty years' service to Hampsthwaite Church, he was followed by Rev. Alec Goodrich, a young man with new ideas, a young man who had been a padre in the RAF. He was a cricket and rugby union enthusiast and had a great interest in drama, travelling around the area with one group and even performing in Ripon Cathedral. He revived Plough Sunday - and the Rogationtide Service, which one year was broadcasted on the radio from St. Thomas à Becket. He also re-introduced the Lammas Feast of the first fruits at the beginning of August. He was a genuine lover of the old traditions. On his horse, Bridie, he used to ride to Felliscliffe to take the service, then come cross-country on his way back home, jumping any hedges and fences in his way.

The fourth Goodrich child, Charles, was born in the village. Mother was a godmother and Sir Cecil Aykroyd a godfather, together with Leonard Houseman and Mr. Averdieck. My father was one of Rev. Goodrich's churchwardens, Sir Frederic the other.

I must mention in passing that at one stage Kathleen's great-grandfather Hardcastle was a churchwarden at our church. In fact, his name was above the door of the old stable, the cause of so much controversy before its demolition in Rev. John Walker's time. Great-grandfather John lived at Heather House Farm, which belonged to Hampsthwaite Church and the rent formed part of the vicar's stipend. He subsequently moved to Saltergate Hill Farm, where Kathleen was born. John's son, Ben, died young - the result, so it was said, of drinking very cold well water on a very hot day, after taking part in a tug-of-war at the Hampsthwaite Feast.

Kathleen's father, Joseph Hardcastle, had to leave school at a young age to attend Knaresborough Hiring at Martinmas (11th November) and there he was hired as a farm labourer. At twenty-one he inherited the farm.

To go back to Rev. Alec Goodrich, he was popular with some of his parishioners, unpopular with others - and eventually he returned to the RAF, where he was happier than in the village.

Next to be appointed was Rev. William Suthern, who came from Huddersfield. He was a different man altogether, being a keen musician. He married Kathleen and me. In his day there were three services on Sundays: Early Communion, Mattins and Evensong. We attended the last mentioned, which fitted in better with our farming life. It is sad that Evensong has lapsed. If ever we go away and visit a church for that service, we enjoy it so much. The "Forsyte Saga" has much to answer for! Rev. Suthern's sermons lasted for at least twenty minutes, which I did not appreciate in my early courting days. We even tried rolling the collection plate down the aisle and other ploys, but all in vain. When Rev. Suthern announced his retirement, my father and Sir Cecil, who had

Joseph Brown: farmer and churchwarden

succeeded Sir Frederic, retired as churchwardens and I was asked to take over. I served the church through two interregna, eventually resigning in 1997.

From Halifax came Rev. John Walker, who, with his wife Jean, moved temporarily into the old vicarage (now The Old Parsonage) until the new house in Church Lane was ready for occupation. In his time the ASB (Alternative Service Book) was introduced, we had our first stewardship campaign, house groups were started, we enjoyed a Parish Day at Barrowby.

Rev. Walker was succeeded by Rev. Tony Hudson, the present incumbent, who came as priest in charge of Hampsthwaite and Killinghall churches and Felliscliffe Chapel of Ease. Now he is vicar of the joint benefice and has been Assistant Rural Dean.

The first organist whom I can remember was Miss Milner. The reading desk was given in her memory. At that time Mrs. Horner played as relief. Leonard Houseman followed and had the position for quite a while - ten years, I should have thought. His repertoire included "To a wild rose". Next came Miss Hall, daughter of a retired vicar from Greenhow, a very skilled organist. Brian Bentley favoured the slow tempo of Rev. Suthern and was reluctant to speed up after that vicar left. After him, in succession came Maureen Swindells, a highly qualified musician, then David Darling from Grosvenor House School at Birstwith. Now we have Ian Haden, who has "filled the gap" so well at a time when church organists are almost impossible to find. For his musicianship and enthusiasm we are truly grateful.

The church choir has had its ups and downs over the years. When the Rogationtide Service was broadcasted on 29th April, 1951, it was well-supported. More recently, when Maureen Swindells was organist, there was for a time a mixed choir of boys and girls as well as adults. Sadly, in this day and age there are distractions for the young on Sundays and the choir has given way to football matches and the rest. Now we find ourselves with only two choir members - George Wainwright, the sexton, who has completed fifty years in the Hampsthwaite Church choir recently and a like number of years as organist at Felliscliffe Chapel of Ease, <u>and</u> June Watler. There are those who volunteer to join them on special occasions, but it would be good to draw on the Sunday School by encouraging the young pupils to take an interest.

I have given a considerable amount of space to St. Thomas à Becket, our parish church, because for me it has played a major part for many years. Now I turn to other aspects of my life of interest and importance to me.

Living in Felliscliffe Parish, I have been active on the Parish Council and have been and still am a governor of the village school. However, because farming has taken up so much of my time both workwise and leisurewise, I have not become involved in the Hampsthwaite organisations.

Edward: Yorkshire Agricultural Adventurer and Show Judge

On the farming front I have been on the Milk Marketing Board Advisory Committee, becoming Chairman of the Yorkshire area. I am also a member of the Yorkshire Agricultural Adventurers, thirty of whom come from each of the old North, East and West Ridings. Five times a year we meet up at the Chase Hotel in York for Lunch, which is followed by a usually stimulating talk given by a top agricultural speaker.

For the present, Andrew has followed in the family tradition by taking over Cote Syke farm in my stead. As for the future, I cannot speak for Matthew. When I was asked in the past about Andrew's career, I used to say that, if he became a farmer, I should "think that he was daft", but that, if he did not, I should be disappointed. Matthew, now sixteen, is taking GCSE this year, followed by Advanced Levels. At the moment, there is an on-going discussion about whether he will go to university or come straight on to the farm. The choice is his. I hope that he will farm, but agriculture has taken a huge downturn in the last six months, the result of BSE and the strong pound. To say the least, it is rather dire at present. It is being predicted that it will be the year 2000 before the pound, the ruling factor, starts to weaken. If Britain becomes a member of the EMU (European Monetary Union), it may help. I just do not know - no one knows. All I can say is that, contrary to two years ago, when the situation was very buoyant and we "had never had it so good", everything in agriculture is now depressed. There was an old saying "Up corn, down horn; up horn, down corn". Usually one or the other was good, but latterly this has not been the case.

I am asked sometimes whether it was a great wrench to retire and move down to the bungalow from the farm. In all honesty I have to say that the time was right, that we were ready to leave Cote Syke and so we looked forward. Besides, I have not really retired: I go up and down every day, I still act in an advisory capacity and I am around at lambing time to help out where necessary. I cannot see myself ever retiring in the true sense of the word, for farming has given me a full, satisfying and happy life.

LIFE IN A VILLAGE SHOP

IN THE THIRTIES AND FORTIES

GLADYS CALVERT
1902-1995

LIFE IN A VILLAGE SHOP IN THE THIRTIES AND FORTIES

GLADYS CALVERT

Looking back on thirty years of shop-keeping in a village store in the Yorkshire Dales, I have so many memories of a life far-removed from present day standards.

It all began when, after eight years of marriage and with a five-month-old baby, we heard of a store for sale in the village of Hampsthwaite. Excitedly one evening we went to view the property with its many outbuildings, orchard and garden. The stock was very limited, but there were drawers filled with hundreds of linen buttons, hooks and eyes and packets of pins; there was a large box containing assorted oils - linseed, lubricating and the rest; there were buckets

```
Spirits ============ Wines

        EDWARD CALVERT
           HIGH STORES
          HAMPSTHWAITE

          Telephone No.
          Birstwith 219

Beers ============ Minerals
```

Edward Calvert's advertisement

and brushes dangling from the wooden ceiling; there was an off-licence with beer at 6d (2½ p) a pint, Guinness, Hall's wine, Invalid Port.

Undeterred, we decided to buy and were promptly told by well-meaning relatives that we should have to "put our backs into it". Being young and enthusiastic, we did just that.

Only one day was set aside to clean up - a dreary, wet day in May. I arrived, armed with brushes and other cleaning equipment, to find my husband on his knees, chipping away layer upon layer of linoleum from the stone floor in the living room. The walls were painted a drab buff colour with a very wide dado of oranges; the doors were a dingy brown - like chocolate exposed too long to the sunshine; the large black fireplace had a high mantel, with a deep plush overhang. Collapsing on to a tea chest, my mother gasped, "Whatever will you do with this place?" Dismayed I may have been, but I rolled up my sleeves and set to work with a will, tackling first the food stores and then one of the five bedrooms.

The removal day dawned, fine, thank heaven. I took a lingering farewell of our first home, then, clutching the baby and a large glass shade, was driven away in state in the furniture van! What chaos followed. There must have been ten people milling about, "helping", but eventually peace reigned, except for the odd creaks - and I grew accustomed to those in time, for after all every old house is haunted.

Each morning was a mad rush. I had to bath and feed the baby before my husband left to seek and deliver orders, leaving me to watch the shop. I well remember my first venture into shopkeeping. A man came for a pint of vinegar. Simple, you would have thought, but I could not find the funnel and his bottle had a very narrow neck. Result? - a flood of vinegar. It was only later that I discovered that the man was totally blind, but could find his way to the shop alone.

Thompson's Garth - better known in the 30's and 40's as High Stores, Hampsthwaite

One day in particular I shall never forget. Glancing out of the window, I saw the orchard full of sheep from a neighbouring field. As they pulled at the blossom-laden boughs of the trees, I dashed to chase them out, leaving the gate open so that about fifty hens invaded the garden and began to scratch in the flower beds. My shouts wakened the baby, who howled lustily - and the shop bell rang!

On the top shelf of the shop stood a row of chamber pots. One special one, decorated with garlands of roses, caught the eye of a dear old lady, who said, "Missus, do you think that yon up theer would fit me?"!! I can't remember my reply.

Some of our customers were maiden ladies, who used to arrive dressed in their rather tall black hats and gloves and bearing flat baskets, covered with newspapers, under which reposed empty Guinness bottles! They insisted upon waiting until the shop emptied before slipping their replacement "tonics, so good for the health" into their baskets.

A hole in the boxroom floor above the shop gave a bird's - eye view of children - and others - stuffing their pockets with goodies when the shop was unattended. We decided to have that room and the next one converted into a large bedroom. The workmen arrived one Saturday afternoon to take down the dividing wall, oblivious of the "peep-hole" until down came a cloud of dust on the irate customer below.

In those days we sold loose syrup. It came in large tins and had to be run off into jam jars by means of a tap. In cold weather this was a lengthy process, so occasionally we left it to trickle into a container. One night we completely forgot that we had done this. My husband went into the dark warehouse and lost his slippers and socks in a pool of syrup.

There was a very large key to the beer cellar and it was a favourite trick of my young son to drop this down a grating, forcing my husband to lower himself through the aperture to retrieve it. Once, his heavy overcoat caught and nearly strangled him. The next time that the key disappeared, he said, "I'll teach that boy a lesson". He tied a thick rope around him and lowered him to the key. I can still see the frightened look on his face - but the key stayed in its assigned place after that.

Next to the shop we had a tiny cottage. This was let to a rather strange woman, who had a permanently fierce expression. She would march up to the counter and throw down her rent book and money without speaking. She had a weakness for dandelion and burdock and would plonk down her empty bottle, saying, "Another"! Truly a woman of few words. In summer she wore a very short, tight dress stretched around her ample form and a sou'wester hat.

Growing up the front of her home was a plum tree, from which a loose branch once dangled over her door. To be helpful, my husband went for a ladder and sawed it off. She was furious, accusing him of taking the branch with her one and only plum. Stick in hand, she was positively dancing with rage, whilst poor hubby was caught by his trousers on another branch in mid-air!

On Sunday morning, 3rd September 1939, as I fed my second baby, I heard Chamberlain's dreaded announcement that we were at war with Germany. That afternoon my husband and his brother started to dig an air-raid shelter in the orchard. The old roof of a Dutch barn was the beginning of another quite sizeable and more comfortable one. In fact, some of the neighbours made a bee-line for it whenever the siren went.

During one air-raid, a nervous man said, "Listen; whistling bombs". It was actually a neighbour's son, coming home on leave. He always whistled "Beautiful Dreamer" to waken his mother when he arrived in the small hours.

We were destined to be more involved in the war. An officer brought us a copy of Army Form B55, which required us to "find Quarters for 12 men of the Lincolnshire Regiment for the nights of 18th and 19th March 1940". It was signed by Stanley Bowen, Billet Master. When they arrived, we put them in the meal house. I asked the sergeant how he would manage to fit so many men into so small a space and was invited to look in when they had settled down for the night. They were lying like the pointers of a clock, feet to the centre - a clever plan.

Army Form B55

In turn, each of the twelve stood guard at the front of the shop during the night. At the appropriate time stones were thrown at our bedroom window, as a sign to my husband - he was in the Observer Corps - that he was to go on duty, German plane-spotting at the highest point on Menwith Hill.

Some troops stationed around the village were known as the Halifax Mashers and they used to give concerts in the Dale Hall. In exchange we taught them to dance to the accompaniment of the Wurlitzer organ.

When my brother came home on embarkation leave, we all went to the Joiner's Arms, which was full of soldiers. They enlisted me as their pianist to play the popular songs of the day. One Irish boy sang so beautifully that I shall never forget it.

The Army Corps Badge

As time passed, evacuees arrived in the village from Leeds and London. They looked so pitiful as they stood in the Village School, clutching their gas masks and waiting to be allocated accommodation. Some eventually grew accustomed to rural life; others did not. During one air-raid, two Londoners came to our shelter. "We're going home", they said. "We'd rather be bombed than bored".

Food rationing added to our work-load. Stocks were allocated on the basis of what was being sold when war broke out. Cutting out the coupons was very time-consuming and the actual counting was a weekend's task.

One day when I was alone in the shop, I heard the familiar sound of marching feet, then silence. In came a sergeant, who said, "Now's the time to make some money, missus". Outside were queues of soldiers, patiently waiting to buy fruit, bottles of minerals and beer. My hands couldn't work fast enough!

Needless to say, there was great excitement once when "Monty" was parked outside in his jeep. Sadly, he did not come in himself, but sent his batman for a purchase.

One moonlit night I heard distant rumbling. As it grew louder, I peered out of the bedroom window and saw a line of tanks approaching from Rowden Lane. Down the village street they thundered and disappeared from sight. I never did discover where they were going.

Time passed, until in 1945 came VE (Victory in Europe) Day. At last we could tear down the blackout curtains from the windows and look forward to normality returning, although, of course, the end of rationing still lay far in the future, as too did our departure from Thompson's Garth in June 1966.

---But that is another story.

REMINISCENCES

ERIC LUNDELL

1906-1995

REMINISCENCES

ERIC LUNDELL

Eric Lundell - interviewed by George Wainwright - reminisces about himself, the village and village characters.

I came to the village in 1916 - in the middle of the First World War. I was nine years old at the time and went to the Village School.

My first job, which lasted for two years, was with Skirrow's at Hampsthwaite House, where I worked on the farm. Afterwards, I served my time with Mr. Fletcher, a painter and decorator, and stayed in his employ until I was called up in 1940. After five years in the army, I returned to the village to find that the boss had "packed in". I decided to start up on my own and "at first it was a bit of a struggle because materials were hard to come by" - but I managed and there was always plenty of work.

One of my jobs was to paint the church clock. The first time I "did it off ladder, although it was about eighty-six feet up: I was a bit younger then"; the second time I got some scaffolding. I also decorated the inside of the church - that would be in Rev. Alec Goodrich's time - and the Chapel of Ease at Felliscliffe, when it was renovated in Rev. W. Suthern's day.

At various times I did work at Arkendale Hall, Birstwith Hall, Hollins Hall and Swarcliffe Hall. It was fascinating to be involved with the gentry in their heyday, although Mrs. Jowitt at Hollins "wasn't a good one to work for: she would tread you down if she could".

I was actively involved in village sport, playing cricket for fifty years and football for forty. I served on the Village Room and Memorial Hall Committees. I remember the Feast with affection: "There was a right Feast once over - part in the Memorial Hall, part on the Green, part in the field where Meadow Close is now. People came from all over for it".

Asked to recall village personalities, he was in his element.

There was "Shaver" Gill, who used to live opposite, and a slater called Wrigglesworth, "a big, tall chap, who lived near the church". In 1928 I bought my house from "Tinner" Wade for £400. At the time it was just a shell - it had no bathroom, no toilet, no

"Ivy Cottage": bought in 1928 for £400

electric light, no water. "Tinner" had a cylinder at the back to make his own carbine gas and there was an "ash pit". Water was collected from the village pump on the Green; electricity came to Hampsthwaite at the end of the 20s. To go back to "Tinner", he had two daughters, one of whom, Mrs. Metcalfe, owned the High Street Stores before the Calvert's. "Tinner" himself was a little man who did all his work in the loft, which he had boarded out and to which he gained access by a ladder.

I remember a village bobby called Alker and his son Jim. The previous policeman, Briggs, was living in retirement by the church when we came to Hampsthwaite and he "did a bit of bicycle repairing in his spare time". His son Alan was a "mate" of mine.

In the early days of cars a certain Dearlove Addyman ran into the pub door. The marks were there for everyone to see for years afterwards. Dearlove was a queer fellow, a real womaniser. He used to organise the ankle competitions at the Feast. He stood all the ladies up on the forms to judge their ankles "by gosh"!

"Saddler" Haxby at work

Another character was "Saddler" Haxby, to whom the lads used to go for bands (= leather) for their "whip an' tops". He persuaded me, Walter Laseby and Alan Briggs to join him as bell-ringers - and "he got us ringing them properly; aye, he did". Mr. Dawson (father of Gerald, John et al.) had a photo of "Saddler", which showed how previously he had rung the bells by himself, with a rope in one hand and a treadle for one foot, as he chimed them.

"Ty" and Bert Pickles lived in one of the little cottages behind Sally Moon's that they pulled down. They were an odd pair. Some lads - including Bernard Wilson - stuffed a sack down their chimney and smoked them out. You should have seen them - black as night. But they never washed anyway!

Sally Moon had the old Post Office - opposite the Corner Shop, where the seat and garden are now - before it was demolished to allow the junction to be widened.

A family called Hebblethwaite lived "up Hollins". The husband worked in insurance; the wife is best remembered for her goitre. She had to wear a black strap around her neck because of it.

John Haxby was a joiner who did much of the carving in the church at the time of the renovation. His son Horace was "a rum lad, who used his fists when he'd had a drink or two". Horace and his wife bought the present Post Office property from a tailor called Pratt, who had traded there.

Johnny Bowers (Roger's grandfather) had his wooden joiner's shop just across the road from the Old Mill - where Peckfield Close is now. There used to be old thatched cottages "top side of Calvert's shop" and Johnny's mother lived in one of them. When the council houses were about to be built, they had to be pulled down.

It was Canon Peck, after whom Peckfield Close was named, who was largely responsible for arranging for the laying of water mains to the village. My uncle by marriage was on the Parish Council at the time and he was against the whole idea.

In days gone by the main jobs in the village centred around the farms, four or five shops, the saddler's, the cobbler's (where Mrs. Bramley now lives and which she bought when it was a draper's), Ralph Robinson's milk business, the Post Office and the bakery (now Spring Garth, home of the Rowntrees). All slaughtering was done at Bridge End Farm before the slaughterhouse was built. Now the abattoir and Robinson's Heating and Petroleum Distributors are the main employers.

Admittedly, there have been improvements, but in some ways the past was better. Then it was unnecessary to lock doors; everyone knew everyone else; no one thought of burglars; everyone was safe. Now everyone locks up; many people use the village simply as a dormitory"suburb"; almost everyone is afraid of break-ins; no one is safe. What a sad reflection of the times.

*Until his health failed Eric spent much time in
his allotment, where he cultivated his prized chrysanthemums*

"OF DAYS THAT USED TO BE"

DOREEN NELSON

" OF DAYS THAT USED TO BE "

DOREEN NELSON

Originally, my father was a collier and my mother a steelworker, but in the mid-nineteen twenties, when times became hard, they left Sheffield for Hampsthwaite. My mother's cousin's husband, father of Winnie Steel, had already moved to Arcadia House on Grayston Plain and was working as a lorry driver for the West Riding Roads Department. As newcomers, my parents lived in a tiny one-up, one-down cottage adjacent to Arcadia House and it was there that I was born in November 1928. Conditions were, to say the least, primitive. I have a vivid memory of the so-called "washing facilities": a metal bowl on an iron stand at the foot of the little stairs!

Winnie's father found employment for my father with the West Riding County Council, cleaning and gritting roads. At first they both walked to the depot at Ripley by way of Ripley Woods; later, when he could afford it, Father bought a motorbike.

When I was four years old, our family - now including a small brother - moved into a rented cottage in the village. It was just off the High Street, up a narrow ginnel, beside which is now the Little House. How things change. Where then there were two cottages, now there is one house, while a derelict little property was converted into "The Casino", the haunt of ladies from Harrogate, who came to play cards and to listen to music. To return to our cottage, it was two-up and two-down, but still without a bath and with a primitive bucket lavatory and midden up the garden.

I went to the Village School and my brother joined me there. At first, Mr. Hough was the Headmaster and Miss Arnison taught the girls dancing, as she rattled her cane. Believe me, the cane played quite a large part in my life - I was often on the receiving end for talking! It is strange what one remembers. I was the lucky possessor of thick, strong hair, single strands of which were much in demand by miscreants, who laid them across the palms of the hands to be caned in order to minimise the pain. By tradition horsehair was used for this purpose, but mine was equally strong.

The playing field behind the school was open for play in the evenings. We had happy times on the swings and on the old wooden rocking horse. In their season, we played with whips and tops, with marbles or with skipping ropes. We had one rope which we stretched across the High Street, where the hairdresser's is now. Traffic was a rare problem then.

Thinking of roads, the High Street was quite wide, but Rowden Lane was a very narrow track. Meadow Close did not exist: there was just a field, where the Feast Fair was held after it was moved from the Memorial Hall land. Peckfield Close had not yet been built. Mr. Horner, the farmer, owned that area and he objected to our playing cricket there. In fact, he would come down upon us with his stick and wallop us!

Back home from school at the end of the day, my brother and I had our evening meal and then we were expected to work on our allotment for half an hour before we went out to play. I was still young when I did washing for Willie Ibbotson. For this I was paid 7/- (35p) a week, all in separate shillings to feed the meter. Originally, of course, - in my parents' time - we had had oil lamps and water had been collected from a pump in the High Street. Only later did gas, electricity and piped water reach the village.

I failed the 11+ examination for entry to the Grammar School, mainly because of a bus drive to Harrogate and because the unknown town itself terrified me so much that I could not even think. Two years later I passed the 13+ for the Technical School at Haywra Crescent and there I learned shorthand and typing - and bookkeeping, which I hated. I became a secretary at 15/- (75p) per week.

Sadly, my mother died of cancer when she was only forty-one, so at sixteen years of age I had to give up my job to look after my father and thirteen-year-old brother. It was not an easy life, particularly as father could not cope without Mother at his side and his personality changed completely. In addition, he had a brain haemorrhage as the result of an accident and suffered several heart attacks.

At one period I worked part-time at Mr. Jefferson's farm at Swincliffe, helping with cleaning, baking and washing. We baked enormous amounts of bread, teacakes and scones with white and brown flour and on threshing day - a particularly busy time, when the neighbouring farmers and labourers came to help - we made dumplings in the copper, in which we had previously boiled the clothes. Of course, it was thoroughly cleaned out first! Another of my chores was to empty all the chamber pots in the house and on one momentous occasion I fell downstairs with my "burden", ending up sitting in it and laughing heartily.

During World War II, I joined the Girls' Training Corps. We trained in the Village Room and paraded to church in blue uniforms. In spite of the wartime conditions young people still had fun, cycling to dances at Kettlesing, Pannal and Norwood. One dark night I lost my handbag at Hell Hole up Rowden Lane and had to grovel around in the dark to find it, not that the contents were valuable, but they were very precious to me.

After a long, unhappy illness Father died in 1947, when I was nineteen. At that age I was considered to be too young to rent the cottage. However, I was engaged to "Tiny" (Herbert), then home from the war after service in several countries including Burma. I must break off at this point to describe how his war medals were all buried in the cottage garden for safety and were never seen again! It is possible that they are lying under the foundation of the garage. But to revert to the cottage - "Tiny" came to the rescue, renting in his name as he was already twenty-five. We went straight from the estate agent's to the Vicar, Rev. Alec Goodrich, to ask him to marry us, as soon as possible. He agreed to

"... straight from the estate agent's to Rev. Alec Goodrich to ask him to marry us"

our request, although it was "strictly illegal" really to marry me without some form of parental consent.

We were married on Easter Saturday, 27th March, 1948, by which time I was nearly twenty. It was a great day. I did some work in the morning, then the ceremony took place in the Parish Church and was followed by a reception at the Orange Tree Cafe in the High Street, where the doctor's surgery is now. "Tiny" had his left arm in plaster after fracturing it, but that just added to the fun. On our wedding night we and a group of family and friends, twelve of us in all, went on the bus to the Wellington at Darley for a drink. We then walked up to the Dutchman at Summerbridge for further refreshment, before returning to Dacre for the Village Dance. Finally, Ralph Robinson collected all twelve of us in his car and delivered us to our respective homes. We, of course, were dropped at our two-up and two-down cottage, where initially my brother - who became a commercial artist - still lived with us. Only later did he move across the street.

At this time "Tiny" was earning £4-10/- (£4.50) a week and he added an extra 5/- (25p) by walking to Crag Hill at weekends and working at the house there. We could not afford a daily paper, so he used to go to the Village Room, where there was an open fire, and read the newspaper which was delivered there. "Tiny" helped me with some of the domestic chores, particularly the washing, which was done in a peggy-tub with a wash-board and a peggy-stick with legs. It was very heavy work.

I mentioned previously my secretarial employment and that at Jefferson's farm. In 1945 I had reverted to a secretarial job at the "War Ag.", where servicemen returning from the war were given small grants. I had also worked at Salk's grocery shop in Commercial Street, before returning to the "War Ag.", where I remained until I was expecting our first baby.

The little cottage - still with its stone-floored kitchen and outside bucket lavatory - became more and more crowded as the years passed. Our sons were born there: Leslie in 1949, Brian in 1952, Alan in 1954. When our fourth boy, Greg, born in 1958, was a year old, we moved to Peckfield Close and I went back to work to help to boost the family income.

I was Home Help to two old ladies in the village, then an assistant at Scatchard's (the grocery shop in the village). I went all over the countryside in their car to collect orders - I was quite a saleswoman. I subsequently became first a cleaner and then a care assistant at the Ian Tetley Memorial Home, where I stayed for sixteen and a half years, loving every minute of it. I worked there in the afternoons and evenings and afterwards "Tiny" and I cleaned the school. I must add that "Tiny's" main job was up the road at Northern Heating, where he worked first for Ralph Robinson, then for Cyril and even later for John Illingworth. When he retired, he was presented with a beautiful engraved glass vase.

On a lighter note, we and our neighbours, the Bartle's, kept two pigs. Once we exchanged a ham and a small amount of money for a decrepit old Austin 7, which "Tiny" rebuilt and painted bright red. I had the doubtful privilege of sitting with him in the distinctly draughty car, while he drove to Kirby Wiske for a new windscreen! And there was another occasion when someone put beer in the petrol tank when the car was parked outside the Sun Inn, causing a total breakdown on the way home.

Turning to the present, I have been doing Bed and Breakfast for about seven years and I enjoy it enormously. I also still help a lady in the village. Sadly, "Tiny" has died and has left a big gap, which it has not been easy to fill. He used to collect old brass, blow lamps and I have kept the collection, polishing and cherishing it. As

"I have been doing Bed and Breakfast for about seven years"

"'Tiny' used to collect old brass, blow lamps"

for myself, I have a number of model cockerels, which decorate the house and to which family and friends are always adding. In my leisure time I am a member of the Wednesday Group and I attend flower-arranging classes, whilst with my companion I go for meals, outings and holidays. I think that I can honestly say that, in spite of early hardships and various moments of great sadness, I am a happy woman.

MY EARLY YEARS

AND

LIFE AT HAMPSTHWAITE SCHOOL

JANET PRITCHARD

MY EARLY YEARS

AND

LIFE AT HAMPSTHWAITE SCHOOL

JANET PRITCHARD

I was born at Clint Cottage in 1941, the second child of a family of two boys and two girls born between 1939 and 1955. My father worked for Mr. Clifford Lister for thirty years, so home for us was a farm cottage. When I was a child we got about by walking, biking or taking the train from the village station, which was conveniently situated halfway between Clint and Hampsthwaite.

I attended the Village School from 1946 to 1953. In the Infant Class my teacher was Miss Slater, a dark-haired lady with a bun. Slates and slate pencils were still in use and I can still remember the awful noise they made. Letter cards and number cards were used to teach letters, writing and sums. Until about 1947 dinner was a packed lunch and I have vivid memories of sitting at my desk, being forced to finish up cold macaroni cheese, although I felt sick! I suppose I was a very tough child in spite of being ill with bronchiectasis (a lung disease leading to many other problems). I have a happier memory of a wall-painting of a woodland and a fairy - it was magical. It had been painted by Miss Slater.

The infants' classroom also housed the lending library, a cupboard full of books not owned by the school, but lent out one evening a week by the librarian, Mr. Rule.

The Middle Class teacher was Miss Arnison. She was "small and very sharp". She used the cane and actually broke one while punishing a boy called Philip Noble, whom she regarded as "the worst boy in the class". He no longer lives in the neighbourhood. Miss Arnison taught us copperplate writing by making us copy curves over and over again until she was satisfied. All we girls were taught to knit garter-stitch and stocking-stitch for dish-cloths. We were even taught moss-stitch - not easy for seven-year-olds. In the second year of the Middle Class, I progressed to making fawn woollen mittens! At eight, we were taught quite complex sewing - measuring, folding, tacking, hemming; embroidery with long and short stitch, cross-stitch, appliqué and blanket stitch. I still have a little bag made at that time to illustrate all these techniques. It's now in use as a Scrabble-tile bag!

The school doctor and dentist used the middle class room. The whole class was moved out while dental treatment was carried out, pupils listening for the moans from the next room. The school nurse visited regularly and did "head-checks" in the girls' cloakroom. I can still remember my mother's horror when I had "fairies" (head-lice) once after a hospital admission.

Playground games included singing games like "King William", "The farmer's in his den" and "In and out the dusty windows". Some games were seasonal: whip and top and skipping with the big rope, two girls turning and several joining in with various clever tricks like "running through and over". Sometimes two ropes were used together. I don't recall any organised games until I was in my last year at school.

The "Big Class" was for children from nine to eleven and sometimes pupils were in that class for three years. Poetry was learned by heart, the class chanting in unison such poems as "Hiawatha" by Longfellow. The older and brighter pupils taught the slower readers. Mrs. Giles was Head Teacher until 1952. She lived in the School House with her husband, who was a builder. Her daughter, Sheila Carlton, now lives in Peckfield Close.

The Vicar was a regular visitor to the "Big Class" and the whole school went to the Parish Church for Christmas and Ascension Day services. The school Christmas Party was held in the Dale Hall Cafe over the present car showroom. The food was provided by our mothers and I recall carefully carrying blancmange in a glass jelly-mould all the way from our cottage at Clint to the party.

At Christmas in 1952 for the first time, I think, we children took part in a Nativity Play. The piano in the big classroom was played for the musical accompaniment. By this time Miss Allen was Head Teacher.

In 1953, Coronation Year, bulbs were planted on the Green by the children. Miss Pyne, who had succeeded Miss Arnison, taught a small group of big girls the Maypole Dance.

In winter, the infants' and middle classrooms were heated by an open fire, which was protected by a guard, while the big room had pipes, heated by a coke boiler. The playgrounds for boys and girls were separated by a high wall, in which was one gate which was either kept closed or was supervised by a teacher. There were three toilets across the playground and two sheets of Izal toilet paper were issued on request! I remember some of the infants having "accidents", which wasn't surprising. Incidentally, in the infant classroom three little day-beds could be opened up for the tiniest children to have a sleep after dinner.

I always had to walk to and from school. The train driver would wave to me and I would see Mr. Fred Horner from Manor Farmhouse delivering milk near the church with his horse and cart. The District Nurse lived where Chris Pill lives now (Gooselea Cottage) down Church Lane - though it was not called Church Lane then: the original name was Church Street. On my left as I walked

Church Lane - originally called Church Street,

to school from the church, I passed an old cottage and barn called "The Temperance", which sold teas. Next came the row of cottages, as now, followed by Addyman's Farm and slaughterhouse, from which animals - after they were killed - were supplied to the area direct. The Saddler's Shop, now derelict, stands in what we still think of as Eric Lundell's allotment. Nearby, was a broken-down gate, long gone, and steps, which remain there in the lane by the School House.

On the right-hand side of the lane coming up from the church I passed the church stable and two cottages, all later demolished. Then, as now, there were the two semi-detached houses, followed by a granary, which was eventually converted into a house (Thimbleby

Close) for Gordon Bailey. After that there was Thimbleby House and a long, high wall up to the old Vicarage, (nowadays know as The Old Parsonage). Also, there is the Old Court, built on Thimbleby's tennis court, as well as Tangfield (Joan Petty's house) and the new Vicarage, both built in the old Vicarage garden, and the Coach House.

To revert to the Village School - we had no school uniform. For me the usual winter wear was a hand-knitted jumper and knee-socks, with a kilt or pinafore dress or wool skirt; for outdoors I had a winter coat, a pixie-hood and a macintosh. In summer I wore hand-made cotton dresses, a cardigan and white socks and - if the weather were very hot - a hated and dreaded sun-bonnet.

Occasionally, when we were in the "Big Class", games were played in the field behind the school, the access being through a kissing gate, now blocked up. In my time there was an old swing frame in the field, but no swings. There was also an old wooden rocking-horse set in cinders and a plank-swing.

Towards the end of my village schooldays, promising pupils took the Scholarship Examination: the first part at school in October, the second part in the following February, when selected pupils were taken by taxi to New Park for the day. I remember a cold, snowy day, a ride round the area with Mr. Ralph Robinson in his brake and arrival at the school, which seemed enormous and very bleak. I was lucky enough to pass the exam and to go on to the Grammar School.

JULY 1952: TOP CLASS AT HAMPSTHWAITE SCHOOL

Back row, left to right:
Mrs. Giles, Brian Hornshaw, Colin Skaife, David Addyman,
Roy Bennet, John Grant, Harry Clough

Middle row, left to right:
Alan Bevers, Mervyn Morrow, Alfred Bickerdyke, Terry Martin,
Gerald Dawson, Leslie Walton, Malcolm Doury

Front row, left to right:
Rosemary Roberts, Rose Martin, Sylvia Bramley, Janet Steel,
Ann Stubbs, Barbara Smith, Rosemary Robinson, Edith Dawson,
Mary Dawson

REMEMBRANCE OF THINGS PAST

RALPH ROBINSON
1905 - 1996

REMEMBRANCE OF THINGS PAST

RALPH ROBINSON

Ralph Robinson, interviewed by his son-in-law, John Illingworth, recalls his experiences in the area.

In 1927 the farming situation was not good at all: there was no subsidy whatsoever; you had to make what you could. The landlord at Bungalow Farm at Clint agreed that I should take the tenancy, providing that my brother - then in Canada - came in with me. The rent was £3 per acre per annum, which was very dear in those days, when a milking cow cost only £25-30. Times have changed.

Claud, eight years older than me, returned from Canada. We both married and went to live in the bungalows, sharing the workload. We took it in turn to do the milking and to take the milk to Harrogate, this twice daily. Then, one day, Claud decided to go back to Canada.

It is strange how things happen. The landlord asked me to share a railway truck of coal and I agreed. My father said that he would have a cartload, as too did a neighbour. That was the beginning of the coal round.

And talking of "rounds", I had a milk round in Hampsthwaite. There were no bottles in those days. The milk was carried in cans and was measured out into jugs with half-pint and pint ladles, at a cost of 3d per pint or 5d for two pints. An old farmer one Sunday said that I had no right to be in the village: "You're a two-faced Wesleyan", he shouted.

At one time I took stone out of the quarry for Pateley Council. It had to be broken by the roadside with hammers, ready to repair the roads.

But to revert to the milk and coal: it was hard work and that's a fact. I'd only one flat wagon then. I would take the milk to the Co-op dairy in Leeds, empty it out, leave the cans for collection later and go straight to the coal-yard to pick up the load of bagged coal. I would bring it back here and "heik" it down, wash, have tea, pick up the night's milk delivery for Leeds and be on my way. At the end of a long day I would return with the empty cans. They don't know they're born nowadays. Only on Saturdays and Sundays did I have a rest from coal! In the end I had at least ten lorries, but when I started with just the one wagon, it was the first time that churns of milk had been taken by road from this area.

Eventually, I turned to tankers and thereby hangs a tale. I took a week's holiday in Scotland and was on the road up to Perth, good farming country, when I met a tanker coming the other way with "MILK" printed on the side. I thought it was a great idea. A little further on, at a crossroads, I saw another one and, as it passed me, I read "SCOTTISH MILK MARKETING BOARD BULK MILK COLLECTION". "That's something fresh", I said. Back home, I contacted "powers that be" in Harrogate and asked for milk tanker specifications. They confirmed with London that the tanker "would require a pump on it, working either from the electrics or from the gear-box". Thus began my venture into tankers and now farmers milk by machine straight into cooling tanks, ready for collection by bulk carriers.

At the outbreak of war in 1939 the village of Hampsthwaite came under Knaresborough Council. As Chairman of our Parish Council I received a letter, in which I was asked to arrange some fund-raising efforts. Everyone in the village was notified of a proposed scrap collection and to my amazement, when the day came, there was a whole wagon-load, including copper and brass. I took it to a fellow in Leeds who had a scrap-metal business and the proceeds of this, together with those from various raffles and whist drives, raised just over £70. Receiving not a word of thanks from Knaresborough Council for the money, I made up my mind that any further fund-raising "would be for the lads when they came back" (i.e. from the war).

A group of us saw a very enjoyable pantomime in Harrogate and decided to go ahead with a production in the village. A female officer stationed at Queen Ethelburga's School (which had been requisitioned by the M.O.D.), who had a dancing school in civvy street, offered to choreograph "Dick Whittington". The performances were given in the school and were such a success that the cast was invited to present it further afield. The profit was shared 50-50 between Hampsthwaite and each of the eighteen places visited. The second year "Babes in the Wood" was performed twenty-two times! "Altogether we got knocking on £1,000, which was a lot of money then".

One day after the war, I picked up the "Yorkshire Post" and read, "Canadian Camp Huts for sale; would suit village institutes, etc". We didn't have a hall then, so I rang Sir Cecil (Aykroyd) and called a meeting. Asked where I'd put it, I suggested the Feast Field, owned by John Smith the brewers. Sir Cecil agreed to look into it and we also had an offer of free transport to the site. I asked Ernest Atkinson to go with me to the camp, which lay five miles from Hereford. On arrival we consulted the auctioneer, who could give no idea of price, but said that "builders were coming down for timber alone - it being like gold-wrapped at the time". We looked around and "saw a good one, with two ends to it - just what we wanted". It had been a recreation hut and we knew that we couldn't let it go, even if it cost twice the £250, which we had agreed would be our limit. Well, the sale took place under an oak tree and the price started at £250! I just kept on waving the catalogue and at £390 I got it"!

> BY ORDER OF THE MINISTER OF HOUSING AND LOCAL GOVERNMENT
>
> ## CATALOGUE
> of
> ## THE SALE BY AUCTION
> (without Reserve)
> to be held at
> ## FOXLEY CAMP, HEREFORDSHIRE
> about 7 miles from Hereford
> ### On THURSDAY, 10th JULY, 1952
> of
> ### 67 SURPLUS HUTS comprising:
> ### 26 Valuable Timber-built Canadian Huts
> and the remaining 41 Huts of the following types :—22 Hollow Brick, 8 M.O.W.P., 2 American Nissen, 2 Nissen, and 7 Miscellaneous Huts.
>
> ### 7 Domestic Boiler Units,
> ### 2 Dish Washing Machines, Hut Fittings
> including —
> 20 Enamelled Baths (5 ft. 6 in.) ; 61 White Glazed Hospital Sluice Sinks ; 6 White Glazed Sinks and 28 White Glazed Draining Boards ; 19 various Galvanised Sinks ; 200 White Glazed and Iron Flushing Cisterns ; Six 40-gallon Farm Boilers; 4,500 ft. of Iron Piping in various lengths and sizes from ¼ in. to 1½ in. (suitable for making iron gates and fencing posts), and
>
> ### about 15 tons of Scrap Iron
>
> THE SALE (which will be held in the Canadian Hut numbered Lot 3) WILL COMMENCE AT 11 a.m. PRECISELY
> and the ORDER of the SALE will be as follows :—Scrap Iron, Hut Fittings, Boiler Units, Dish Washing Machines, Canadian Huts and Miscellaneous Huts.
>
> AUCTIONEER :
> # T. A. GOSLING
> F.A.L.P.A.
>
> **ARRANGEMENTS FOR VIEWING**—The Lots may be viewed between the hours of 9 a.m. and 5 p.m. from Mondays to Fridays, and between 9 a.m. and 1 p.m. on Saturdays.
> A PLAN of the Site at the rear of this Catalogue will assist Viewers to find the various Lots, and an Attendant will be at the Main Gate to render any further assistance.
> **LIGHT REFRESHMENTS** will be available on the day of the Sale.
> **AUCTIONEER'S OFFICES :** 1, Offa Street, HEREFORD. Telephone No. 3175.
>
> PRICE SIXPENCE

Front of the catalogue of the Canadian Camp Huts' Auction

Back at Hampsthwaite I saw Charlie Haxby and Alan Powers, who agreed to help to transport the hut from Leybridge. At the camp we took the tiles off first, then dismantled it in sections, marking each one. "It was a right job". A week later we set off for home. By then Sir Cecil had purchased the Feast Field (the present Memorial Hall site) from John Smith's, so the hut was dumped in the field in heaps. Eventually it was erected by the villagers.

The hut was dumped in the field in heaps

There was a group known as the "Yorkshire Tykes". One played the piano, another was a good, straight singer, the third was a comedian and the fourth played a one-stringed fiddle. "By gum, they were good". I asked Nellie I'Anson at the pub whether she would put on a dinner which, together with an entertainment by the "Tykes", would be organised for the "lads (i.e..those who had been in the armed forces) to come back to". The menu included rabbit - five of 'em - which everyone thought was chicken!, and the "Tykes" performed for a tankful of petrol, still rationed at the time.

When the lads were asked whether they wanted to share the money raised from the pantomimes among themselves, one of them, Willie Ibbitson - he's dead now - proposed that it should be used to equip the hall. That was what happened. Sadly, it was burned down later.

The repairs to the roof were necessary because of severe gale damage in Spring 1962

So our thanks must go to all those who were originally responsible for making a village hall possible: to Sir Cecil Aykroyd, who gave the site, to Ernest Atkinson, to Ralph Robinson himself, who had the vision, to Ricky Averdieck, who was involved in getting the loan from the Government and this on a prefabricated building, which had never been known before. Ricky later procured a grant - for which Ralph Robinson went down to London - for the present Memorial Hall. We must not forget also those villagers who gave of their time and their talents in its erection - and those who by donation paid for the trees around the site, planted "in memoriam".

J.I.

MEMORIES ARE MADE OF THIS

WINIFRED M. STEEL

MEMORIES ARE MADE OF THIS

WINIFRED M. STEEL

I came to the village when I was eight and a half years old and have lived in and around Hampsthwaite ever since. I was born in Sheffield in 1916 and was effectively an only child, as my younger sister was born sixteen and a half years later. My father, a bus driver in Sheffield, changed to different work when we came to Grayston Plain to look after a sick uncle in 1925. Uncle retired from Arcadia Farm to a house in the village opposite the Chapel, which he bought for £400. The family stayed on at the farm. I had been accustomed to seeing buses and the occasional ambulance, driven by my father; now there were cows and a pony and trap.

Father initially worked as a road-man for Knaresborough Council, occupied mainly in the Pennypot area, but on Wednesday afternoons he swept the road at Hampsthwaite from the church to below the bridge. Later, he drove lorries for the Council, doing such jobs as gritting, tarring and snow-ploughing. In those days, after using the snow-plough the men would go back and clear the gateways of the wells of the snow that had been thrown up. Whatever the weather, Father was not allowed to take his lorry home, but had to walk to and from the depot at Ripley from Grayston Plain.

I myself walked to school in all weathers and never missed a day from enrolling at eight and a half to leaving at fourteen. Believe it or not, I was the only child who possessed wellington boots, which had been bought in Sheffield for "the country". At first I caused consternation among my friends by walking in the beck in my boots.

There were three classes at school, the Upper Fourth Standards being together in the big room. I don't think that very large families were in fashion then. One of my first tasks was to learn "proper" writing and to forget the "printing" that had been in vogue in Sheffield. I also had to learn The Lord's Prayer. Early morning assembly was followed by the usual lessons: Scripture, English, Arithmetic, History, Geography, Science, Drawing and Sewing. The last named I particularly liked and I was very good at it. Sewing lessons were enlivened by the teacher singing songs from "The Tales of Hoffman" in an excellent contralto voice. I also learned to knit - and we all had to produce socks in brown wool. A few of us girls had to go to the vicarage to learn special dances for the garden parties held in the large garden there. Canon and Mrs. Peck looked after us well, providing afternoon tea.

Canon and Mrs. H. J. Peck and family
Standing: Gordon (left) and Victor (right)
Seated: Gwen (left) and Geraldine (right)

We were taken on Nature Walks, some of them around Swincliffe. We played in the "river field" - now closed to the public - beyond the bridge on the left. That field belonged to Mr. Clifford Lister, an important farmer. Both boys and girls played a game not encountered elsewhere. Called "Touch and pass", it had similarities to Rugby. We did not compete against other schools in this sport, but we did play opponents at cricket and football. Wednesday was games day - a highlight of the week. Sometimes there would be punting on the river after school.

The head teacher for most of my schooldays was Mr. Hough. Previously, he had been a captain in the army and he brought new ideas to the school, introducing drill for fifteen minutes before dinner. In the days of his predecessors, an elderly, old-fashioned couple, the only exercise we had was throwing bean bags!

I carried my dinner to school in a small attaché-case. In one of the cottages opposite Manor Farmhouse lived a kindly lady called Miss Ada Ellis, who had one leg in a calliper. At a charge of sixpence a week she would make a drink of tea for eight or nine of us and would warm up our food. She also made cakes for us - three for a penny. Then, from foreign parts appeared a cousin, who married Miss Ada and took her away. After that Mrs. Hough made tea, which she served in elegant china cups.

When I left school at fourteen, there were only fifty-two pupils in the school and some of the top class, Standard 7, were allowed to stay on until Christmas, instead of going at the "official" time in July. Just two years later poor Mr. Hough died at the age of forty-three. His widow survived to the ripe old age of ninety-two, living in a house in Hollins Lane.

My family attended the Saltergate Hill Mission, where there was a non-sectarian service on Sundays. It was much easier to

Saltergate Hill Mission

worship there, rather than walking all the way to the Parish Church in Hampsthwaite.

I recall one serious illness from which I suffered: I had congestion of the lungs at thirteen years of age. Dr. Clarkson from Birstwith visited me and recommended linseed poultices. I was fed on eggs whipped in milk and my friend Doris's mother, who lived nearby, made a fatless sponge.

I first met Eric, my husband, when I was fourteen. His family moved to Hampsthwaite from Haverah Park, where his father had been a farm labourer. From an early age, Eric and his brothers had done unpaid farm work each morning before setting out for school. When he started real work as a farm labourer at fourteen, Eric weighed only five and a half stones, having just recovered from rheumatic fever. He had spent six months in a hospital in Liverpool, to which he had been taken by horsedrawn ambulance. Why Liverpool, I wonder?

But I digress. I was nineteen and busy working for an aunt with a broken leg when Eric started to court me. He was then working for Mr. Fred Horner (a tenant farmer of the Aykroyds from Birstwith Hall), at Manor Farmhouse. He lived in, worked from 5.30.a.m. to 7.30.p.m. and was paid half-a-crown a week.

For thirty-four years Eric and I lived at Clint in a tied cottage owned by the Listers. In the course of sixteen and a half years we had four children, of whom Janet (Pritchard) was one. Eventually, the long hard days - milking the cows, ploughing, hay-making - took their toll and Eric moved to another job at Octavius Atkinson's, the steel firm then based at Starbeck. There he was put on the steel guillotine "temporarily" and stayed on it for eleven and a half years - until his retirement!

In my early days in the village there were more shops than now. The Post Office was opposite the Corner Shop at the Joiner's Arms junction, but was moved to its present site in the High Street when the original building and the neighbouring cottage were demolished to allow road-widening. Incidentally, in the cottage lived a strange man called "Ty" Pickles and his nephew. "Ty" had long, grey hair, a beard, huge boots and a walking stick - a frightening sight. Bertie, his nephew, had a black beard. These were the famous two who were smoked out when some naughty boys put turfs over their chimneys!

The Old Post Office opposite the Corner Shop at the Joiner's Arms' junction

Gladys Bell's husband sold boots and shoes in his shop up the High Street, where Gladys still lives. There is little sign now that the building was a shop, except that one of the windows, where the boots and shoes were displayed, is larger than the others.

Later, there was a haberdashery and clothes shop run by Elsie Bramley. It was opposite a cobbler's and those two shops eventually swapped sides of the road. Mr. Hopkinson, the cobbler, would repair any shoes which I left on my way to school immediately, so that they were ready for collection on my way home.

There was a greengrocer in the Corner Shop premises, a grocer - Mr. Gill, who also ran a taxi - at Lonsdale House below the Post Office and a butcher called Mr. Jackson, who took meat around in a high dogcart. Up the High Street there was another grocery store - which the Calvert's later owned - run by Mrs. Metcalfe and her sister. Sometimes I would call in for four ounces of yeast after school and had great difficulty in communicating with Mrs. Metcalfe, who was stone-deaf. In the house now known as Spring Garth there was a bakery, the baking being done in what has now become Brookroyd Garage.

Services came late to the village. I remember various pumps, one on the Green and one in Mr. Horner's farmyard. From the latter two girls from the school would collect water every day. Up at Arcadia Farm twenty-six buckets had to be filled from one pump and carried into the farmhouse each day. Washing was done in a copper and peggy-tubs.

Hampsthwaite Feast used to be held in the Feast Field, where the Memorial Hall is now. The first hall was an army hut brought over in pieces from Hereford in 1951. Mr. Ralph Robinson and Mr. Clifford Lister organised the transport and Eric drove one of the lorries. That hall burned down and was replaced by the present one, the foundation stone being laid in 1966. Mr. Robinson, Mr. Lister and Mr. Ernest Atkinson were all heavily involved, whilst Mr. Adrian Walmsley, a business man, who was treasurer, went to London for grants.

The Women's Institute was started in the "Guide Room" over the present garage at "The Hollies" and was in full swing by 1948.

I have happy memories in spite of early hardships. Janet, our daughter, says that she never heard Eric and me complain about being hard up and we even managed some luxuries like piano lessons for Janet and one brother.

I REMEMBER, I REMEMBER,

THE HOUSE WHERE I WAS BORN ...

GEORGE WAINWRIGHT

I REMEMBER, I REMEMBER,

THE HOUSE WHERE I WAS BORN ...

GEORGE WAINWRIGHT

I was born in Hampsthwaite in 1917 at a house opposite the parish church, next door to the Lamb Inn (it being then a private hotel called "The Temperance" and kept by two old ladies called Miss Kirkham and Miss Thompson). At the time, my father was fighting in the Battle of the Somme and was wounded. When he came home at the end of the war, he was employed by the Greenwood's at Swarcliffe Hall as groom and chauffeur, having been groom for the Mountgarret's at Nidd prior to 1914.

I was brought up mainly by my grandma, spending all my weekends and spare time with her. It was a happy part of my life.

"We used to go to church on Sundays, Grandma and I"

We used to go to church on Sundays, grandma and I. She had one of those old stone hot-water bottles and she used to knit a cover for it once a year in heather mixture wool. That kept the bottle warm and we used to sit with it between us in church on cold winter days. Grandma lived in the village a long, long time and died just after World War II. In her will she requested that I should play the organ at her funeral - and I did, at the service in Thornthwaite Church.

Hampsthwaite was very quiet in those days: there was hardly any traffic that I can remember. Apart from Canon Peck, who by this time (1922) had a second-hand Austin (Heavy) 12 Tourer, I don't think that anyone in the village had a car - there were only horses and traps and carts. Dr. Ashby, the local doctor, who lived at Thimbleby House, was one of those who went about in a pony and trap.

In the house on the bridge side of the Temperance Hotel lived a gentleman called Busfield. Even for those times his seemed a rough old property: there were stone floors with no coverings at all and a small coal fire; gas, electricity and water were to come later. At the back of my grandma's garden, if I rightly remember, was the only water supply for that row of houses - provided by a pump. Also outside were the old earth closets and to light our way to them in the dark we had to use lanterns with candles in them. Beyond the garden, along a path and round a corner were red brick toilets. That was until the church got the car park and then they were knocked down, thank goodness.

I mentioned Thimbleby House before. Well, another of the buildings opposite was the old stable, which had been erected in the 1800's. When visiting clergy came to preach, they put their horses in there; the mowers were kept in it and the old parish bier, now up at Felliscliffe. There was a real rumpus when it was pulled down. Its original stone plaque is still down in the church cellar.

The village policeman in the 1920s was Briggs, a wonderful man, highly respected by the local community. He took many a young lad in hand, cuffing him behind the ears and making him behave himself. I recall a mate of mine, who had a bike which he used to ride at night without a light. I think he had a girlfriend up at Killinghall. On one occasion Briggs was waiting for him when he got there, took the bike and lamp from him, and told him that he could walk home until he learned to behave himself. He never did it again. You see, that was a much better punishment than nowadays, when lads are brought to court and just laugh in the face of the judge, when they get off with a warning or a small fine.

There was a real character who lived next door but one to my grandma, a strange old lady called Mrs. Wilks. She always wore a black frock with a lace collar and a white kerchief edged with lace on her head. I'm perfectly certain that I was once told that she had worked for the Royal Family as a bed-maker. She used to say that she ate ground nutmegs to keep herself healthy. Whether they did have this effect or not I don't know, but she persevered with them, grinding them up, soaking them in water, then dripping them. Horrible! As a lad I used to go around to see her and to have a natter for half an hour, but fortunately I never had to taste her nutmegs!

"Slater" Wrigglesworth was another character. He used to look after the church roof and it used to take him ages to send the bills. I never did find out why. He was a tall chap, who lived in the house ("Ashley House"), which the Travers' own now.

Next door to "Slater" was the local butcher, a great lover of sport. He, Dearlove Addyman and Tommy Moon were pals and used to umpire the local cricket matches. When it came to the Feast, a great occasion, Dearlove, who was a bit of a ladies' man, would always give a piece of ham for the sports, which were then held in the cricket field. He would put the ham on an argent pole, blindfold

"Dearlove, who was a bit of a ladies' man ...used some long benches for a Ladies' Ankle Competition"

all the ladies, start the race, move the pole, then help them to find it, having a bit of a cuddle in the process! He also used some long benches for a Ladies' Ankle Competition. Amidst great hilarity he would go along the row, feeling all the ankles to decide which were the best.

After the sports, "Parson" Peck, for thus he was affectionately called by the villagers, would go out on to the field, bearing a big black bag, which contained all the money, and he would give prizes to the winning competitors. Afterwards, there was a big "sit down" tea for us in the school. Aye, they were wonderful times.

When I was a little lad, it never crossed my mind that one day I would be the Feast Sports Secretary, but there it is. That position was held by Willie Ibbitson, who was called up about the same time as I was and who suffered terribly in Burma. He was missing for six months and was cruelly treated by the Japanese. He was never the same again and died not long after the war - a great loss to the village. He had a good bass voice and sang in the choir for many years. He was a great chap... aye... but there it goes.

Ivy Cottage, on the left of the village green (coming from Church Lane), where Eric Lundell lives now, was once the property of "Tinner" Wade, a local tin-smith, who repaired pots and pans. As a lad, I went with my grandma to the sale that was held when he died. That must have been in 1927-28.

"Jeffreys ... lived part of his life at Hookstone Garth, shown on old maps as Hookstone School Farm"

I well remember Jeffreys, who always kept some very thin mutton bones in his pocket. After a pint or two at the Feast, he would put them between his fingers and rattle them. Actually, he could keep quite good time as he danced on the village green, the local lads and lasses topping him up, as it were, with a drop of ale! He lived part of his life at what is now "Hookstone Garth", but which is shown on old maps as "Hookstone School Farm". I am describing, by the way, the house at the bottom of Swincliffe, where one road goes left to Hampsthwaite Head and the Robinson's and the other right to Swincliffe Top: it is the house on the corner there, built in about 1666. According to the "Return and Digest of Endowed Charities for the Parish of Hampsthwaite 1896", the farm was part of the endowment of Hookstone School near Thornthwaite. The relevant document reads as follows: "A freehold farm at Hampsthwaite, containing 6a., 3r., with a house, barn and outbuildings thereon, let to Charles Jeffrey on a yearly tenancy at the rent of £21".

... But I have got ahead of myself. Let us return to Rowden Lane and to the Old Mill, which in my younger days was two houses. That property, together with the two cottages at the bottom of the lane and an acre of land (where the four bungalows stand now), was bought by an old gentleman called Ball for just over £500! That would have been just after World War I. As to what all that would be worth today, well, I just don't know. Incidentally, if you look at the cottages, you will see that they have been modernised, but they are still very low at the back, having been thatched, single-storey dwellings originally.

I can still picture Hampsthwaite when there was just the old part of the village: no council houses, no new developments, just open spaces. Yet the village must have been fairly busy in the past. After all, there were three pubs: the Bay Horse at Swincliffe Top, the Joiner's Arms and the Lamb Inn. Many of the footpaths that we walk on Thursday evenings (from the second week of April to the first week of September) were direct paths to pubs. If one had lived, say, at Cruet Farm in Hollins Lane, one could have picked up the path from there, have gone through the fields into Rowden Lane and have crossed that road and the field opposite to the path at the bottom of Swincliffe, which would have brought one out eventually almost at Swincliffe Top and the Bay Horse.

I mentioned our Thursday evening outings. We find it very interesting to walk these old footpaths in the parish. We know them as those who drive around in cars all the time can never hope to do. They just do not realise what there is to see in the local countryside, both nature-wise and history-wise. What a pity! I do wish that more people would become involved with these walks. Meanwhile, as a group we stick together: we are a happy crowd and we have enjoyed this glorious hot summer of 1994 so much, as we have soaked up the beauty around us.

One day, perhaps, someone will edit this tape for me, so that the contents can be kept in an archive or used for local reference. Thus, this knowledge, much of which only I now seem to have, will not be lost to posterity.

A WALK DOWN MEMORY LANE

BERNARD WILSON

1919-1998

A WALK DOWN MEMORY LANE

BERNARD WILSON

Enter the Family

Father came from up the Dale and his family was in the public house business. They had the Black Bull on the Skipton Road, the Old Oak at Low Laithe - and the Dusty Miller, at a time when the Scar Dam was being built up there. My parents were married from the Old Mill - the Mill House - in 1910. They had a smart military wedding, one of the biggest ever in the village, my father being in the army at the time.

My eldest sister - now eighty-four - was born in 1911, the first of three sisters and four brothers who arrived at three-yearly intervals, making it very easy to remember all the ages. I was born in 1919 at the top of the High Street in what was then a little farmstead.

Looking back now, I cannot imagine how we all fitted into the tiny house. There must have been three of us in each of two bedrooms and the youngest in the main one with our father and mother. Of course, there was no gas or electricity laid on until the 1920's. We had to use oil lamps and beautiful many of them were, with a brighter light than some of the present-day bulbs. To light our way to bed we had candles. As its source of heat every bedroom had a fire, but this was lit only when someone fell ill. In such a crisis neighbourliness really counted and it would not be long before someone would arrive, bringing jelly and custard, bananas and sweets. It was worth the suffering to be able to enjoy such goodies!

At home all we youngsters had jobs. When I was only eight years old I was responsible for the water-carrying. I had to fetch enough first thing in the morning to last all day: in fact, I had to fill a great earthenware pot. This process was repeated in the evening.

Our house backed on to the Cockhill Beck and every so far along there were steps down to the water. This was where everyone had to come to collect a supply for clothes-washing and other domestic chores. Drinking water came from the three pumps in the village - one at the top of the High Street, one on the Village Green, one down in the "church farmyard".

And so to School

Until I was fourteen I went to the Village School. Some children came from as far away as the Army Camp, walking all the way. In those days Rowden Lane was very narrow, very wooded, very dark and little ones from the age of five had to walk down it from the Skipton Road. There were the Walton's and the Ireson's and, from Grayston Plain, the Harris family and the Harper's.

In winter, when we arrived at school, we had to line up in the big classroom for doses of cod liver oil and ginger biscuits. At break in the morning we had powdered milk at a halfpenny a cup.

Nearly every year - holidays apart - we had as long as six weeks off, this on the instructions of the Medical Officer because of outbreaks of infectious diseases like diphtheria and scarlet fever.

We had regular visits from the "nit lady", who used to come to inspect our hair, whilst at home our mothers used to put newspapers on the table and "attack" our heads with a smalltooth comb. If we were infected, and we usually were because head lice spread so rapidly, our mothers would "crack" them between their two thumb nails. Revolting!

At eleven, I passed one set of exams for the Grammar School. Unfortunately, I was ill when the time came to sit the second part and the chance to further my education faded. To compensate, because I was very artistic, I was lucky enough to go to the Art School in Harrogate to learn sign writing.

School was enjoyable on the whole and I ended up as Head Boy. Evelyn Walton, Madge Baren and I were presented with books by Mr. Hough, the Head Teacher, whose son Richard was a bomb-disposal expert during the war. My book was called "Rovering to Success" by Baden Powell.

Out into the big, wide World

Because I could not take up an apprenticeship until I was sixteen, I spent two years after leaving school at Hampsthwaite House Farm. This was owned by a Scots couple called Skirrow, whose son John was at university and who, in vacations, would come down into the village with a string of lambs - just like pet dogs - which he looked after. A great sportsman, he fell ill and died from pneumonia. I worked as a farm-labourer on a very low wage, but with a quart of milk as a daily perk. I started at six o'clock in the morning and at hay time and harvest rarely finished before eleven o'clock at night. I helped with every aspect of farm work except ploughing, single row ploughing, with the horse pulling the plough complete with its ploughshare (the detachable part which cut the under surface of the sod from the ground). The farmers bred their own cattle and, when the animals were ready for slaughter, they were taken to the local abattoir. There was not all the buying and selling that one sees at cattle marts now. When cows were milked, the liquid was poured through a sough (drain) into open cans. Hygienewise such milk would not be acceptable today, for the law demands that it goes through pipes into the tanks and is hermetically sealed.

--- But I digress. There was also a poultry farm, where I was expected to feed the chickens and collect the eggs. In the house itself there was a big restaurant, so for weekends we had to dress chickens, geese and turkeys, which were all included on the menu. Ham was also served, their own pedigree pigs being slaughtered to provide this. Customers came from as far away as Scotland to dine

One of Bernard's signs:

"Customers came from far and wide to dine on this restaurant's fine fare"

on this restaurant's fine fare. We have tried in vain in the village to trace any surviving members of the Skirrow family, because of some land here which belongs to them.

Almost all boys leaving school were employed as labourers, some in farming and some in building. Odd ones like myself, who wanted alternative work, went into Harrogate to train as mechanics or to become errand boys for market traders. We all used bicycles because there was no other means of transport. I was lucky enough to have a job that was just that little bit better than the norm: at Topham Bros., one of the largest firms, with a permanent staff of one hundred and twenty. I started as a sign-writer, one of thirteen, at a penny-ha'penny per hour for a forty-four hour week, including Saturdays. On special holidays like August Bank Holiday Monday and Tuesday and Christmas Day I had to go into Harrogate, taking all the posters which we had produced to advertise the next week's films and displaying them around the town. There were no neon lights then, no plastic letters; everything was done by hand. I worked on almost every house on every street, for in those days each property was individually named on the doorpost or gate. In fact, I could stand on any street corner, knowing that within minutes something that I had painted would pass by!

For King and Country

On 3rd September, 1939 I was down in the village outside the little shop, waiting for war to be declared. I was called up into

For King and Country - "I was called up into the Infantry"

the Infantry "with three lads from up the Dale" and was in the army for seven years. I served in Iceland, Egypt, North Africa, Sicily and Italy - at the time of the invasion - and it was there that I was taken prisoner. I actually escaped, but was recaptured and was in a holding camp when Lord Harewood was brought in. The German guards swore that they had caught the King of England! It was in that camp, as an NCO, that I did my first tunnelling and, believe me, it was the most frightening experience of my life. As a result, when I came out of the army, I suffered from claustrophobia: I could not even go in a lift. Incidentally, we did surface at the end of that tunnel in a tobacco field, but someone "spilled the beans" and it all came to naught. My third escape took place in Germany. Recaptured yet again, I expected to spend some considerable time in solitary confinement. Imagine my surprise when, three days later, we were moved and went on what became known as "The Big March", which ended only when we met up with the Americans after the German guards deserted.

Back to Blighty

On my return to England I had a brief leave before reporting to the Intelligence Corps Headquarters at Aldershot. It was from there a year later that I was demobbed and travelled north to Harrogate, where by chance I was picked up by one of Ralph Robinson's milk wagons. Thus, I arrived back in Hampsthwaite "in state" to find a huge "Welcome Home" banner draped across the bottom of Finden Gardens. It was wonderful to be back in the village again.

Village Memories: the Buildings

Between the wars the village was self-supporting. Almost every trade was represented: tinker, tailor, saddler, builder, painter, baker. There were some very good shops. I lived right opposite High Stores at the top of the High Street. It was like an Aladdin's cave with everything from chicken feed to medicine, treacle to paraffin.

Another general store, in the centre of the village, was owned by a Mr. Gill, who also had a petrol pump there and a little garage, which had previously been the Band Room with a stage. As kiddies we used to go down there, hoping to hear the big drums, which between practices were suspended from the ceiling with all the other instuments. Whatever happened to all of them I don't know. The said Mr. Gill also had a charabanc, which he drove into Harrogate once a week.

When buses started to run up the Dale, it was found that they could not turn at the High Street-Hollins Lane junction, so the old Post Office, opposite the present corner shop, had to be pulled down to make way for road improvements. So too did a cottage between Roger Bower's home and the farm to allow wider access to Birstwith Lane.

There were three pubs and three cafes. One of the pubs, the Lamb Inn down by the church, was owned by an auntie of mine, who took it over when it was "changed". Previously, when some of the clergy came on their horses to take services, they would preach, have a little drink, preach again, then have another drink. At the end of all this they were not always fit to ride home so, until they had recovered, their horses would be put in the parish stable, since demolished in controversial circumstances. The "change" which I mentioned came about when the name of the pub was altered to the

"Temperance Hotel" to indicate that intoxicating liquor was no longer being sold. Instead, morning coffees were served.

One café, run by the Smithson's in the house until recently owned by the Budden's, faced Lonsdale House, while another was in the present Post Office building. On Sundays we would go to church. I was head choir boy in the days when we were paid a penny for each service and practice and for two memorable visits to sing in York and Liverpool cathedrals, under the direction of Miss Peck, our choir-mistress. Afterwards, we would set off for a walk, during which we would meet other families similarly occupied. The roads seemed to be packed with people, some of whom would halt for a breather at the cafés, if they were open.

There were three butchers over the years, the last being a Mr. Jackson, who had his business down by the school in the house where the Edinger's live. Then, he used the front room as a shop; now I don't think that "the powers that be" would allow such a practice.

"The abattoir has always been here and cannot really be moved from its present spot"

The abattoir, as run by Mr. Addyman, has always been here and cannot really be moved from its present spot. In the past all the buildings around it were part of a huge farm, while the abattoir itself was solely for the locals in the village. Of the other slaughter houses, one was up near the Dale Hall and I used to go there on Mondays and Tuesdays to help my uncle; the main one when I was a child was down at Bridge End Farm, over the bridge and down what we called "the cinder path" on the right. I rather think that there was a family there called Dearlove, some relation to the Addyman's, hence Dearlove Addyman's name.

Brookroyd Garage was originally a farm, taken over by the Bowers, and along the front, where the present showroom is, there was a building like a shack with a corrugated iron roof. It was there that they used to carve the gravestones. As kids from school we used to stand and watch them.

Housewise things have altered. I can remember when the only brick houses were those built about 1923 opposite the Methodist Chapel. The only other little bit of brickwork was between the Joiner's Arms and the Post Office: there were four cottages there, of which two were knocked down and replaced by a brick building. The older part of Hampsthwaite, stretching from the bridge along Church Lane, past the Village Green and up the High Street, really does go back into history, being part of the original Roman Road from Ilkley to Aldborough.

Yes, there have been many changes since I was a boy. After the war, the villagers wanted to build a Memorial Hall in memory of the lads who did not come back and to celebrate the return of the rest who did. Sir Cecil Aykroyd did a deal with John Smith, who owned the field where the present Memorial Hall now stands. In exchange for that field the brewery was given a piece of land at the back of the Joiner's Arms - an amicable arrangement to all concerned.

The shops gradually started to disappear - as too did the station and railway line, Hampsthwaite's pride and joy when they came into being in the late nineteenth century. Eventually, we ended up with the Corner Shop, the Post Office, one slaughter house which, like Topsy "just growed", two garages and the pub.

Village Memories: Entertainment

In the past, of course, there were no televisions, so we had to make our own amusements. As it cost fourpence-ha'penny return by bus to travel to Harrogate, jaunts there were out of the question on our wages. Instead we cycled everywhere and often on Sundays a crowd of us - as many as a dozen boys and girls together - would head for Fountains Abbey for the day.

Between the wars there were very good men's and ladies' sections of the British Legion to organise events: concerts, Sunday band performances on the cricket field, the Christmas Fair - to mention but three. There were some really hard workers, including my father, who was involved in a big way, and my mother, when she had time to spare from her duties as the local midwife and layer-out of the dead, hospital worker and collector of the pennies, which entitled those subscribing to hospital beds when they were sick. Later, Hampsthwaite, as we know it today, was in the hands of organisations.

The main "entertainment centre" was the Village School. At Christmas, for example, a pantomime was presented in the main room and, strange as it may seem, all the villagers managed to squeeze in, despite the stage - stored at the old vicarage between times - taking up a considerable amount of space. There was no Dale Hall then and the Village Room - or Reading Room, as it was called at that time - had a billiard table, which took up much of the floor area, so that it could be used only for small whist drives.

Dale Hall

There were two tennis courts at the back of the present Dale Hall and they were much in demand. A football team played games in a field on Hollins Lane now occupied by houses. Because of a cash flow problem the matches faded out, only to be resurrected about ten years later when money from whist drives and other functions became available for kit and other expenses. Nowadays, there are four teams in two leagues.

Occasionally, the British Legion Committee would organise an outing to some seaside resort; the Church always had a choir trip - very popular with the choir members; the Chapel had a picnic by the river, where we paddled. Access to the river-bank was later prohibited, which was sad for all those who found such enjoyment there.

Of course, there was the annual Feast, a big event in the village calendar, with its roundabouts and fair engines. One of the latter was made in 1914, one in 1916, and both are still operational, though only used for exhibition purposes. I recently repainted the livery on them. Sometimes there were three fields full of merry-go-rounds and other delights - and one year they were even on the Village Green.

A Changing World

How different life was in the past. We have moved a long way from the days of ponies and traps, sit-up-and-beg bicycles and Mr. Gill's once-a-week charabanc trips into Harrogate; from the days when a close-knit, self-contained community found its work and its entertainments on its own doorstep. Now there are endless cars, motorcycles and a reasonably regular bus service; now a "dormitory" situation has developed: the building of more and more houses has led to the introduction of a peripheral population, which departs for work early in the morning and returns home only in the evening. Furthermore, the latter group is for the most part transitory, promotion and growing families causing constant movement from first-time-buyer homes. Yet the situation is not wholly bleak. Some "incomers" have integrated over the years and have made their own active contribution to village life.